GHOSTS IN THE LANDSCAPE

VIETNAM REVISITED

To the memory of Victor Lincoln Crump
and the men of Charlie Company

GHOSTS IN THE LANDSCAPE

VIETNAM REVISITED

Photographs by Craig J. Barber
Essay by Alison Devine Nordström, Curator of Photographs,
George Eastman House, International Museum of Photography and Film

UMBRAGE EDITIONS

GHOSTS IN THE LANDSCAPE

Visuality, Memory, and the Shaping of a Generation

by Alison Devine Nordström, Curator of Photographs, George Eastman House, International Museum of Photography and Film

The cultural memory of every historical period controls vocabularies of specifically nuanced words. This shared language, like the shared experience it reflects, can turn the names of places into nothing more than the singular events that occurred there. For many, Gettysburg, Paschendale, and Iwo Jima are less places than they are only incidents of wars, devoid of other contexts, histories, people, and culture, frozen in time. For those of us who turned eighteen the year of the Tet offensive, Vietnam is one such word. We may know it to be a place, we have a sense of its climate or cuisine, but in our hearts it remains a war. The place name Vietnam summons only a few fixed images: a hurt and terrified running girl; a summary sidewalk execution; a bloody soldier reaching out to a fallen comrade; a helicopter balanced on an impossibly populated roof. The people I know who were there when these pictures were new own them too, along with more personal ones that may never have become photographs: a rice field seen by a face four inches above the water; a jungle from which dangerous people may emerge at any moment; a village in flames. They tell me both kinds of images endure, even now as they are becoming old men. They often come at night, unbidden.

Craig Barber knows both kinds of pictures. He was an eighteen-year-old marine from a village in upstate New York when he found himself in Vietnam forty years ago. He stayed there for twenty months, rarely knowing exactly where he was or the larger logic of what he was being told to do. He wasn't a serious photographer then, though he had been taking pictures since he was a kid and he carried an instamatic with his combat gear throughout his tour of duty. It wasn't until the mid-1970's, after a period of angry and aimless knocking about so characteristic of those times and that generation, that he realized he could make a different kind of imagery, and his distinctive visual vocabulary began to emerge. In 1987, Barber began a series that would come to be called "Dream Gardens," an emotionally evocative sequence that confidently demonstrated the power of his counterintuitive compositions, photographic tricks of scale and quiet mastery of technique. In "Succulent Gate," improbable semperviva appear to loom towards the camera before a soft pattern of fruit trees and fence. In the equally disorienting "Tulips," the sharp light and shadow on foregrounded pointed leaves and buds just becoming blooms gives them a stature that belies their scale and outweighs the mysterious window behind them. Barber's more recent work, too, made in Havana and in the liminal woodlands of rural New York State, demonstrates the delicate dance between beauty and uneasiness—the vital balance between fascinans and tremendum, document and introspective journey.

In 1995, Barber made the first of three return visits to the battered and distant country where he had come of age. Quietly and tentatively he began the series of photographs that became *Ghosts in the Landscape*. In a remarkable personal investigation of both place and psyche, Barber finally produced these profound and dreamlike images that may, for him and some of the rest of us, ultimately stand beside, or even replace, the bloody and horrific images we carry inside us that reduce Vietnam to a place of perpetual guerrilla war. They are provocative images, challenging us to look hard, without our usual preconceptions. Still and slow as they are, they suggest an imminent scream of fear or anger beneath their apparent tranquility. There is calm and resolution in these pictures, to be sure, but there is also residual horror and the acceptance of it that comes at last with maturity, and sometimes becomes wisdom.

Barber works with a variety of pinhole cameras he has made himself. The simplest of objects, they are essentially dark hollow chambers holding a piece of film that is exposed for some minutes to the light entering from a small hole. The process cannot be fully controlled; vagaries of light, timing, and circumstance lead to serendipitous outcomes. Their softly darkened corners and rudimentary out-of-focus forms lend these photographs a sense of the archaic and the mysterious. The long exposure time blurs any elements of the image that move, turning branches into feathery gestures and people into wraith-like traces in an eternal landscape.

Barber produces large negatives by this straightforward technique and contact prints them in platinum on thick and textured watercolor paper, sometimes singly and sometimes several to a page. The tonality of the platinum process produces stunningly rich blacks and a full spectrum of delicately nuanced shades of gray. The contact print renders astonishing detail, the precision of which contends with the ambiguity of the pinhole image. The diptychs and triptychs, in particular, provide both an enveloping grandeur of scale and a further feeling of fragmentation and dislocation. The result, a poetic mélange of the crude and the impeccable, is beautiful, edgy, contemplative, and disturbing. His images are ambiguous. They are less informational than emotionally redolent. Slow and pensive, they focus our eyes, and, indeed, our breathing, on a single moment, and a single still space.

Barber's Vietnam work shares these characteristics with his earlier series, but its perfect melding of evocative subject and expressionist process and medium make it especially worthy of our consideration. There are more than forty photographs here, each stiller than the next, depicting fecund and flourishing countryside, still and empty water, spare traditional dwellings, and more imposing French colonial structures from the decades before Bien Den Phu. In " We Entered Another World" (plate 21), a diptych unites prints from two negatives and the two halves of a simple bridge stretching from a clear sun-dappled foreground on the left until it disappears at the other side of the right hand frame into a wind-tossed tangle of broken fronds, trunks, and undergrowth. In its mystery and calm, it is compelling but also somehow ominous, as though Eden were already tainted with knowledge of the Fall. The bridge itself, as the image's central formal element, as well as the picture's title, remind us that this work is about passage, not only the passage through space that characterizes the movements of both soldier and photographer, but the passage of time that marked both the young man's battlefield coming of age and his tentative integration with the older man he became. Despite the compositional joining of the bridge's two parts, the physical structure of the diptych halves it irrevocably, obviating any complete unity. Past and present link, but imperfectly, in much the way we simultaneously grasp and fail to grasp the fragments of our youth that we remember. Similarly, in "Everything has a Purpose" (plate 1), two prints side-by-side offer a rhythmic and sculptural assemblage of bundled-cut palm frond ribs against the rooflines of primitive dwellings, under a sublime yet apocalyptic sky, underscored by clouds stretched impossibly by the film's long exposure. The intensity of such an image (made over much more time than that in which we usually see) is transformative. The photograph stops us; framed, the content makes us consider it as we would not were we actually present at the scene depicted, as Barber could not have when he first confronted the sights and smells of Southeast Asia. Fittingly, this picture enjoys a perfectly ambiguous title, both an admiring and immediate observation of the frugal use—everything culture of traditional Vietnam and a deeply philosophical acceptance of a past experience that can be further understood though not amended.

If Barber's diptychs embody dichotomy and fragmentation, his sweeping triptych "Temple of Literature" demonstrates the narrative and accumulative power of the larger format. The three equally-sized elements work standing alone, but together constitute a remarkable left-to-right progression. The viewer's eye rests first on a discrete and static mangrove tree, centered in its own frame, roots intricately entwined to suggest time and multiplicity and to stand as a whole made of parts. In the center, a remarkable building, with a doorway as dark and impenetrable as any of Atget's, looms from the back to the front of its frame with exactly the mass and gravitas of the tree. On the right: synthesis—a fragment of temple abruptly connecting to the centered architecture and a receding irrelevant, balancing assembly of trees on an infinite plain. What is this place and what does it mark? Is this a memory of the past or a shoring up of fragments against—or for—the future?

Craig Barber is a tall, worn man with a lined face and gentle smile. From time to time, the line of his back and the set of his shoulders recalls the young marine he was once, but there is usually little suggestion in his manner of the visions he carries of a nearly incomprehensible time and place. As he has journeyed through the decades and the miles since his first encounter with Vietnam, he has recorded his growth and healing in works of art we can all access. Made in the duration of several heartbeats, these pictures look like dreams imperfectly remembered. By sharing not only his vision but the process he has undergone in finding and expressing it, Barber takes us all towards some other Vietnam, far and near from the place we pictured when we were young.

RETURNING

I began returning to Vietnam early in 1995. My intent: photographing, writing, and learning about the land I first saw as a combat marine many years before. Full of youthful ignorance upon my initial arrival in Vietnam, saddened and still ignorant upon my departure, I returned home with more questions than answers and more anger than I care to admit. This time, older, gentler, and more mature, I hoped for a better understanding. Carrying vivid memories—some good, some not so, all intense, all needing clarification—I navigated each day through the landscape of my emotions.

Craig J. Barber
2005

Plate 1

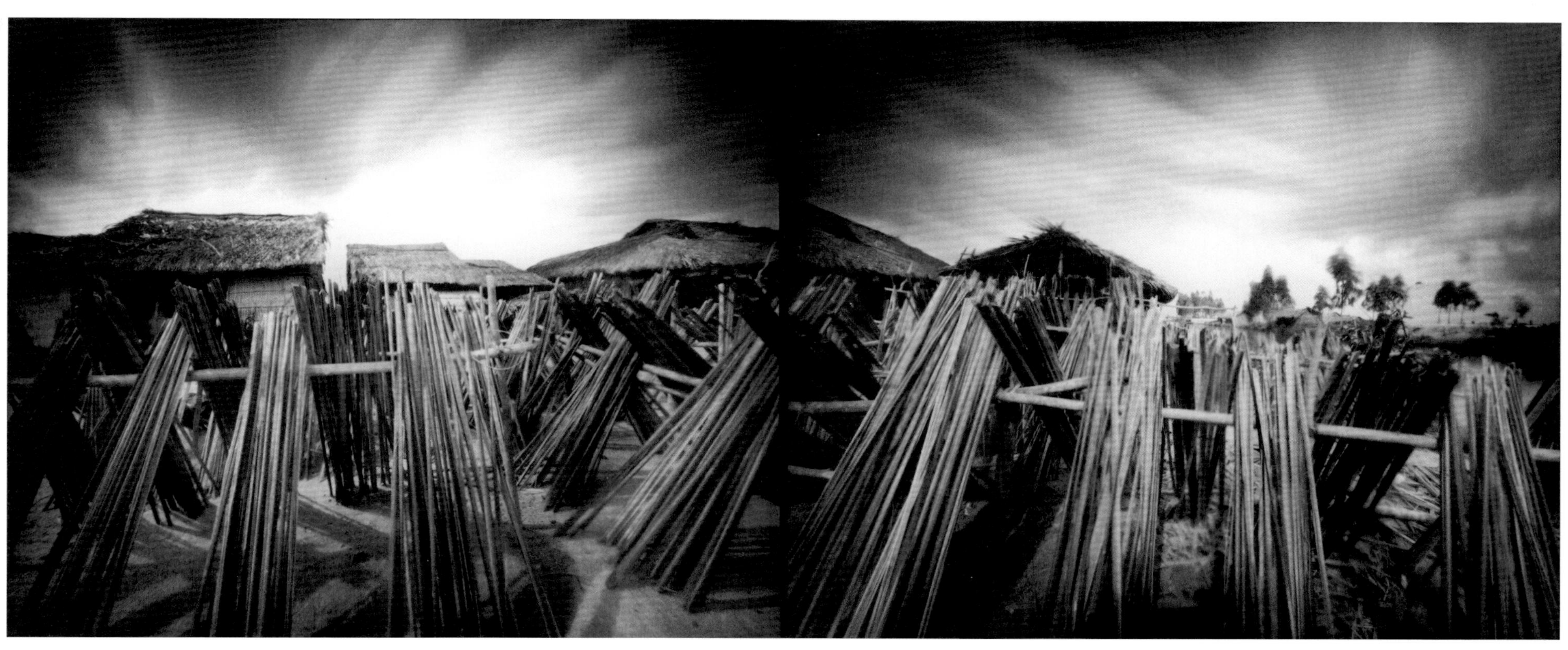

Plate 2

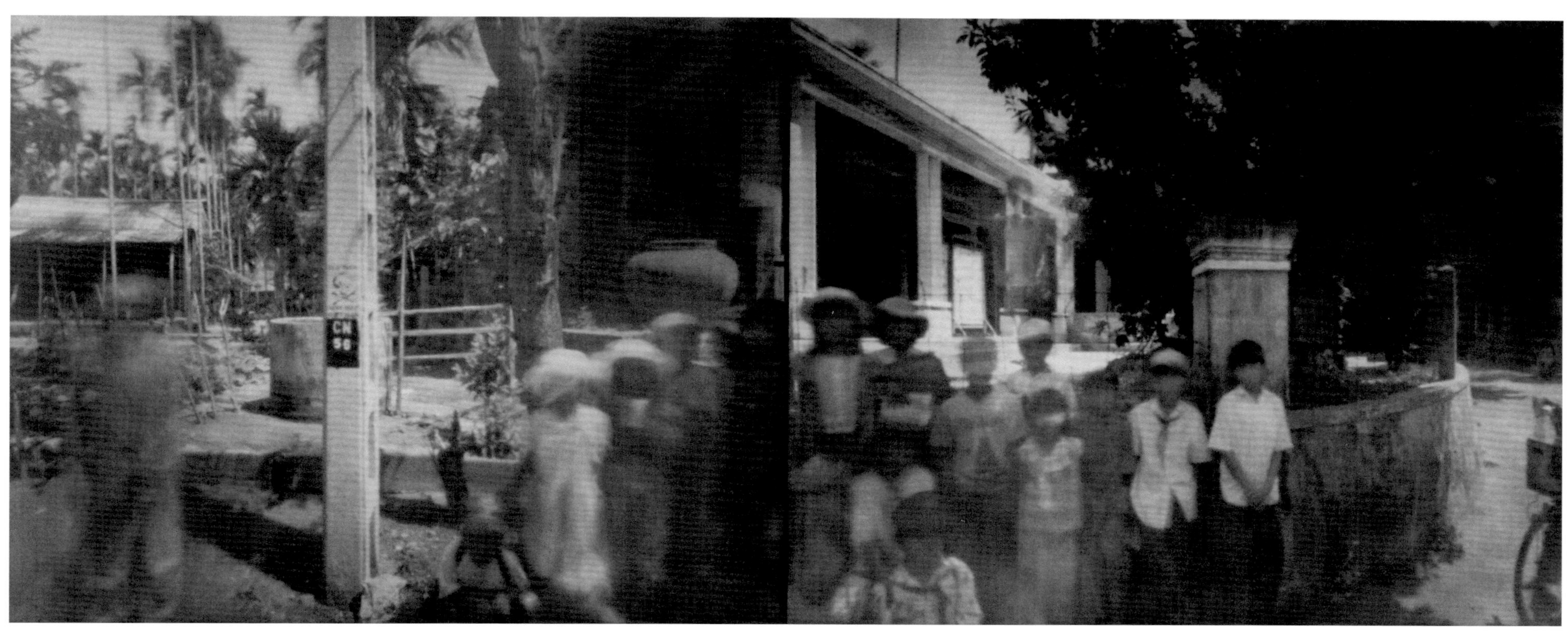

Plate 3

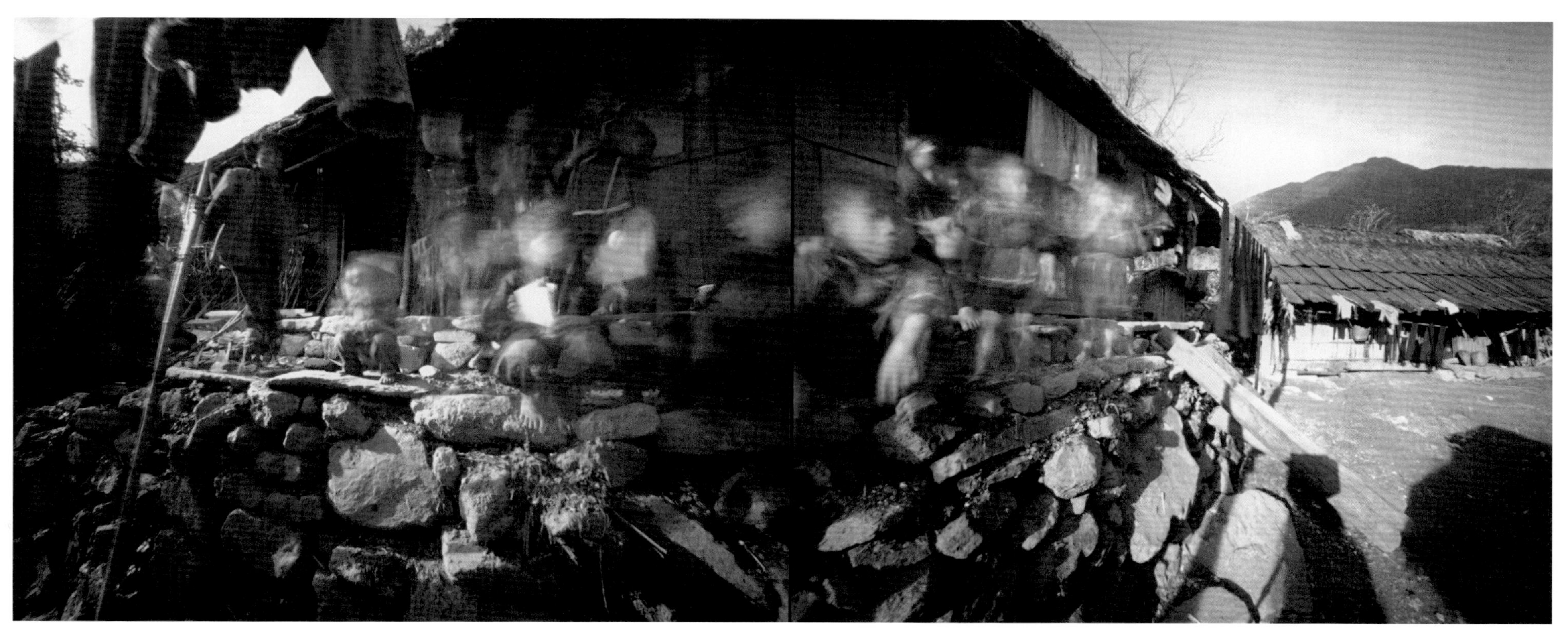

Plate 4

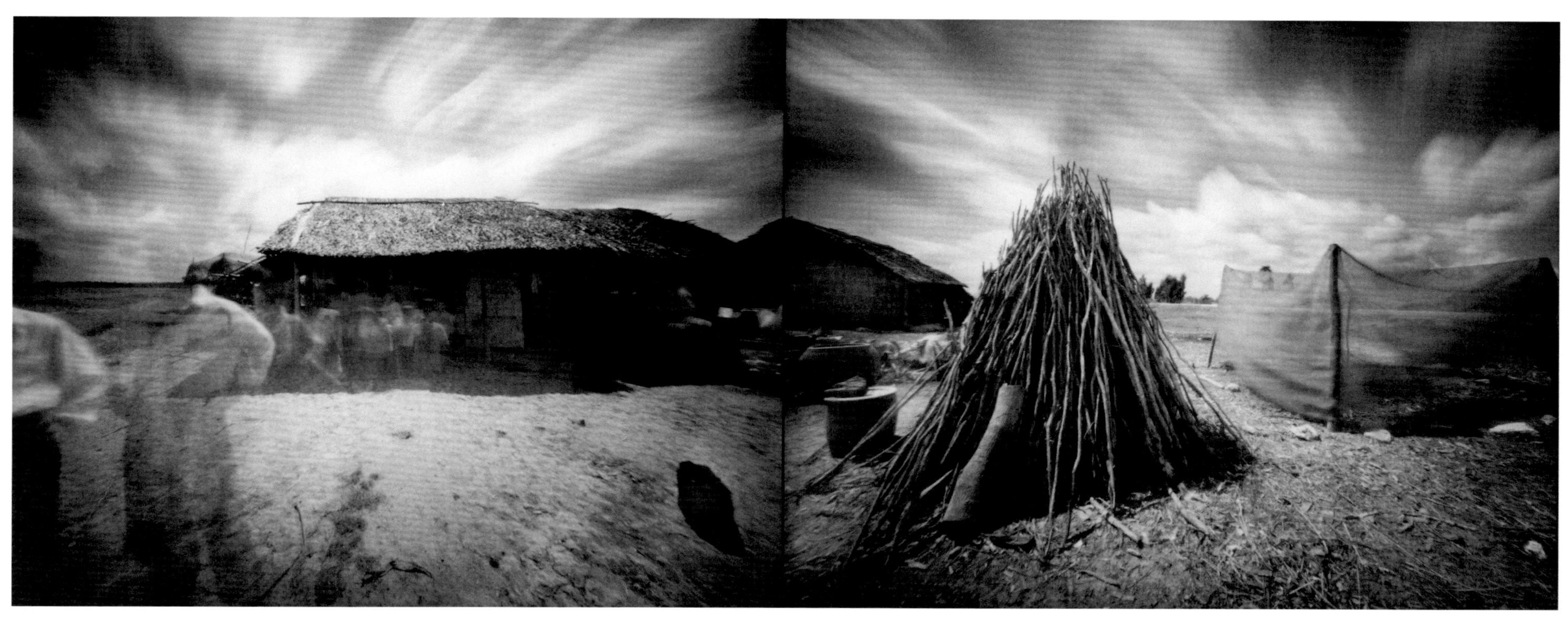

Plate 5

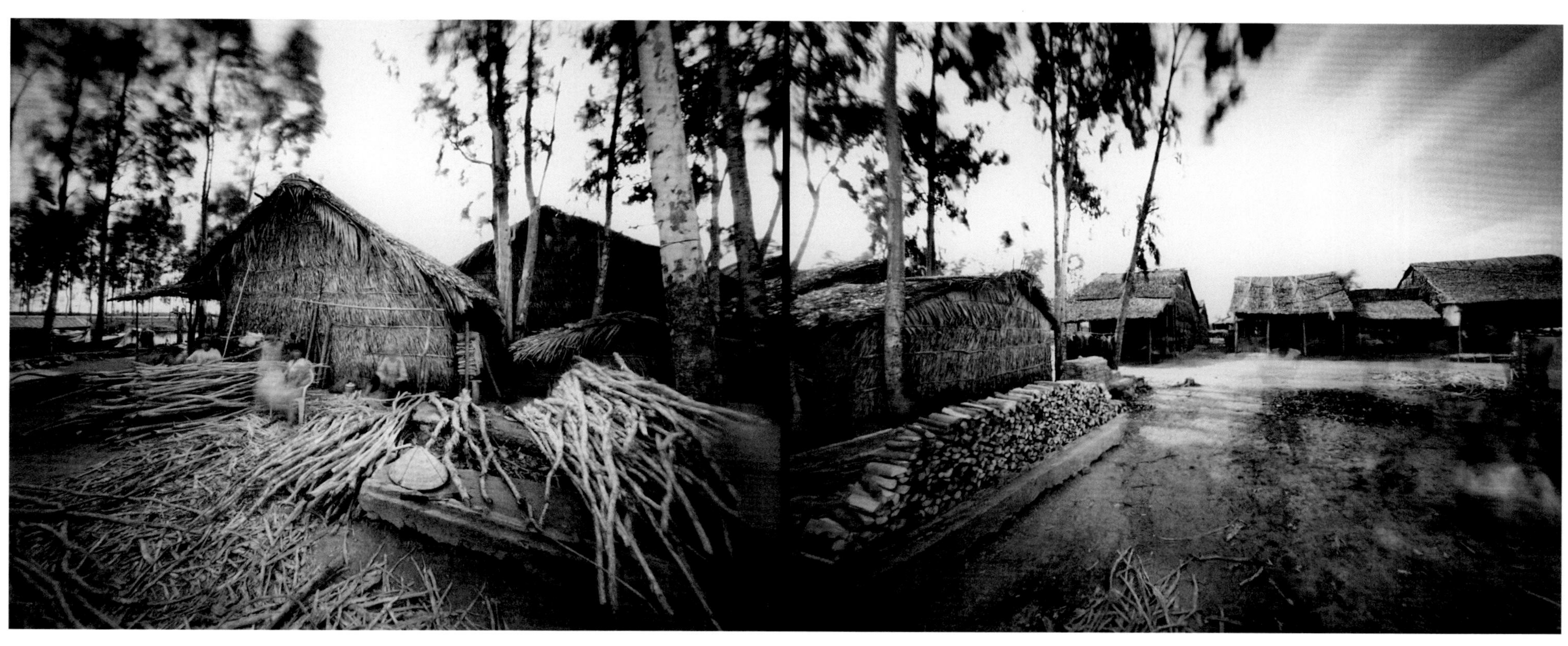

Plate 6

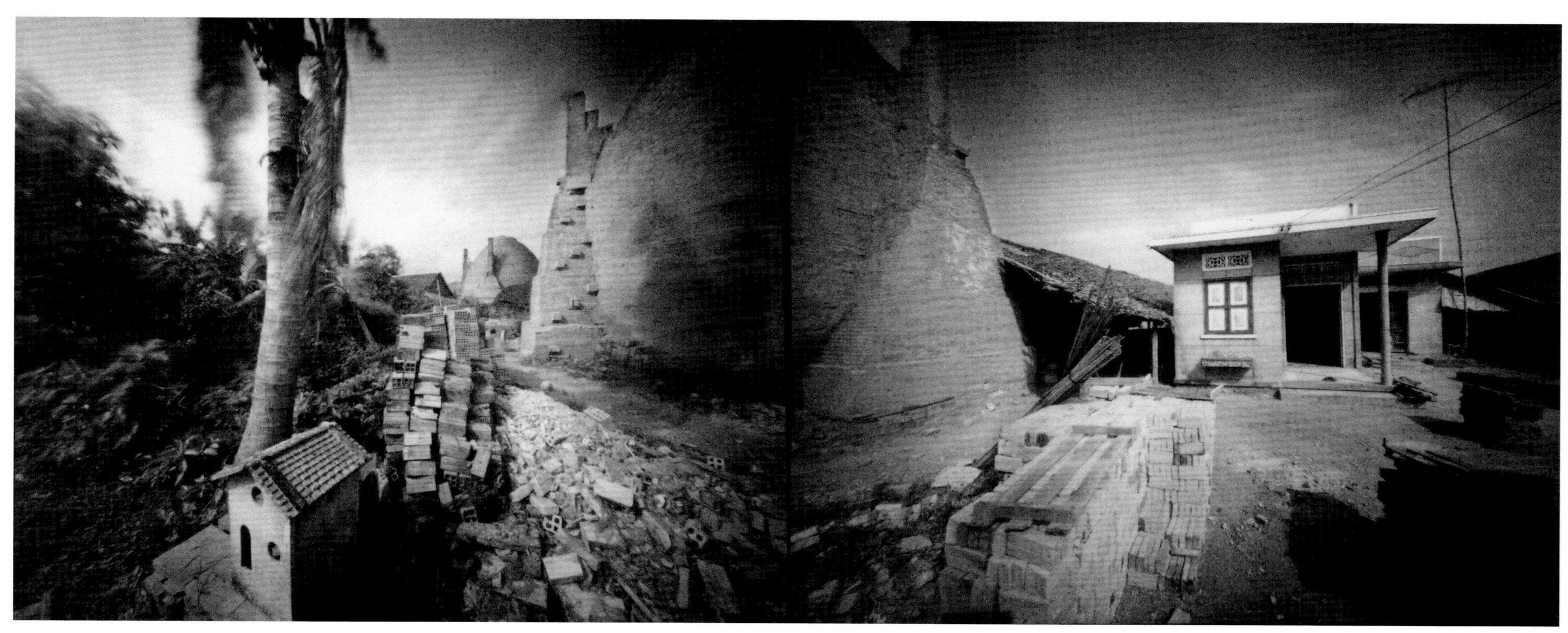

Plate 7

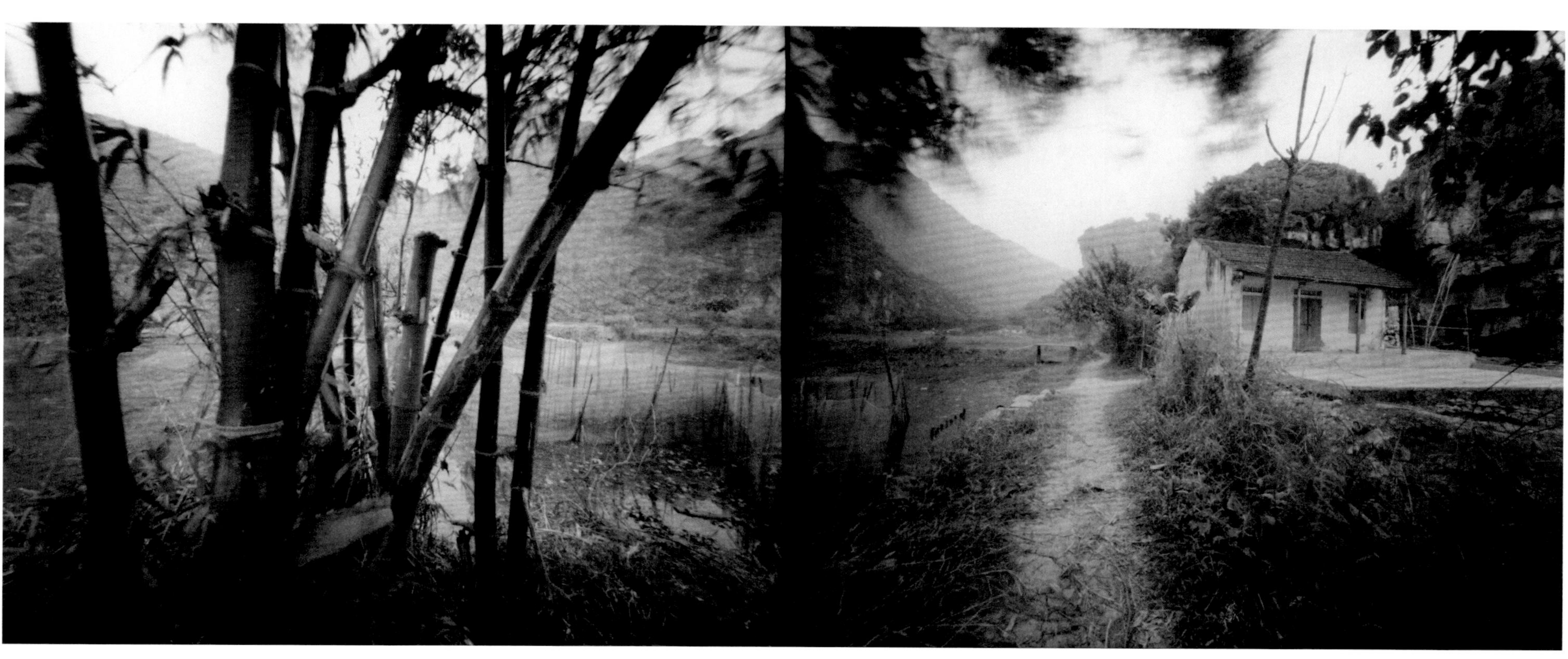

Plate 8

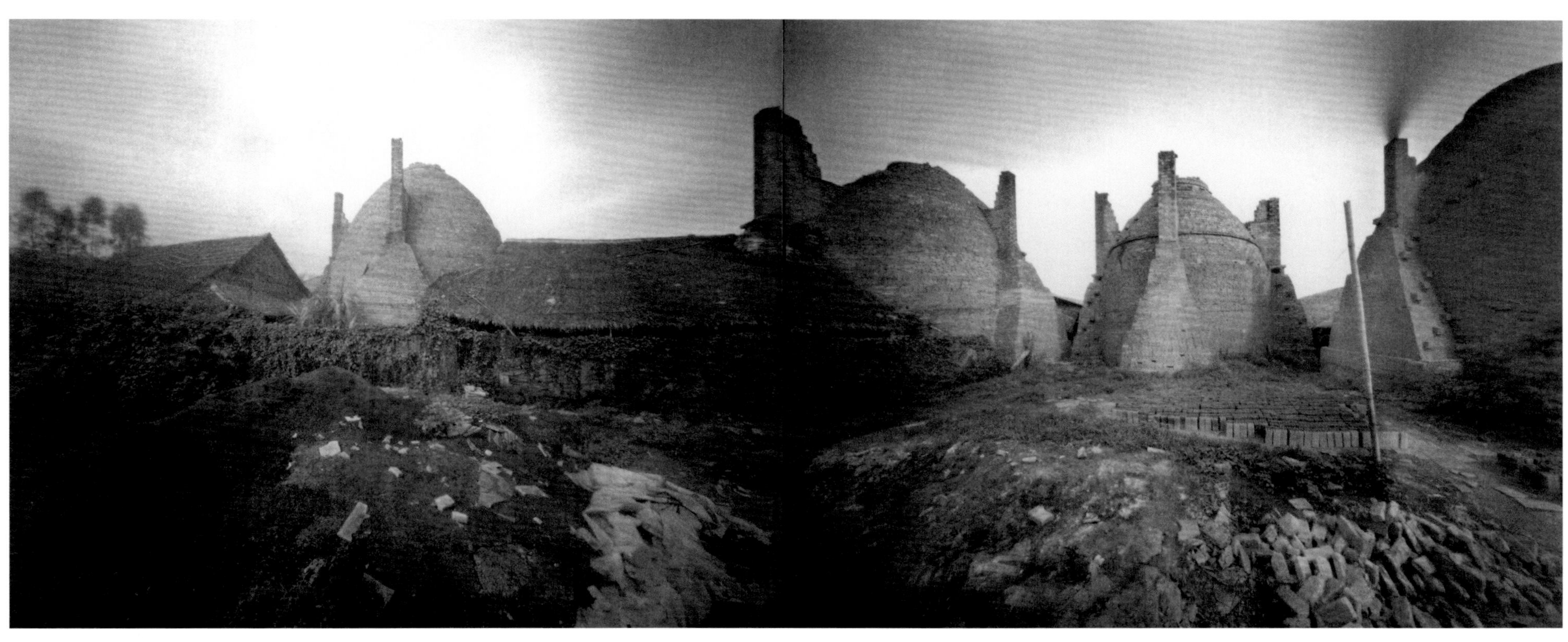

Plate 9

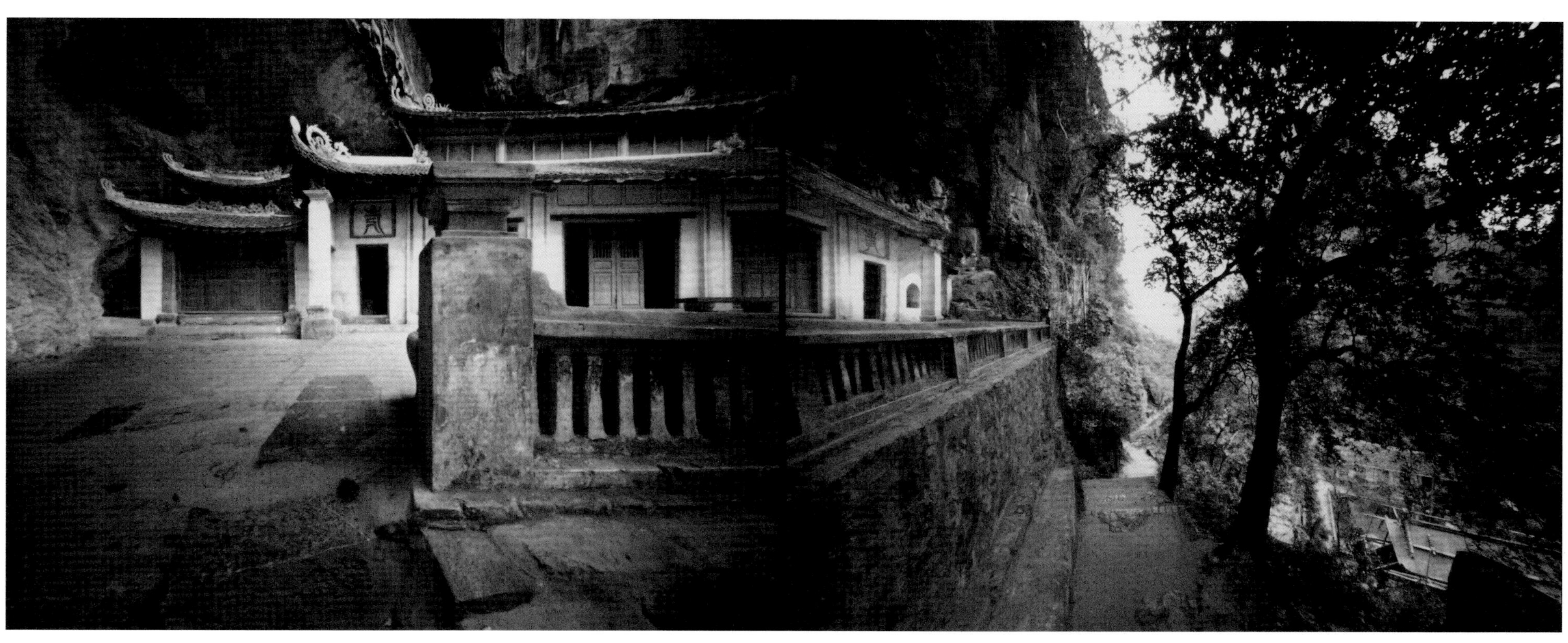

Plate 10

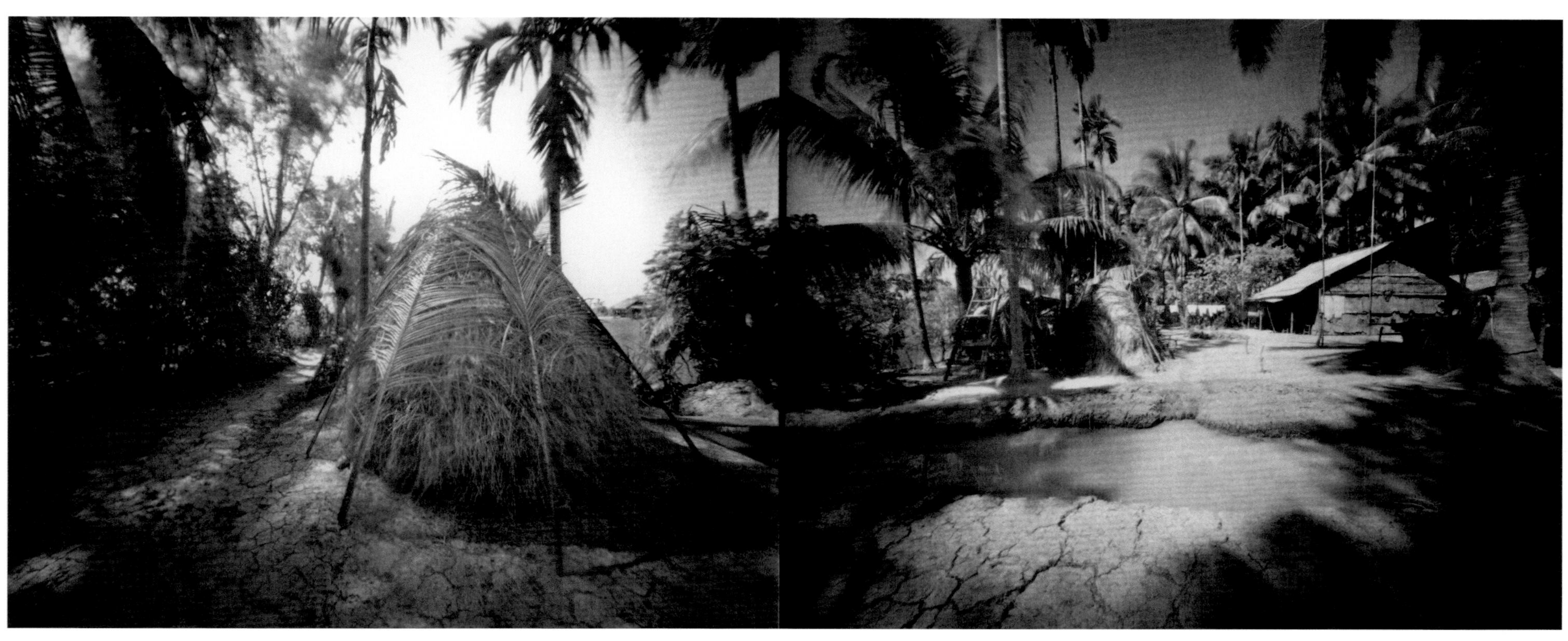

Plate 11

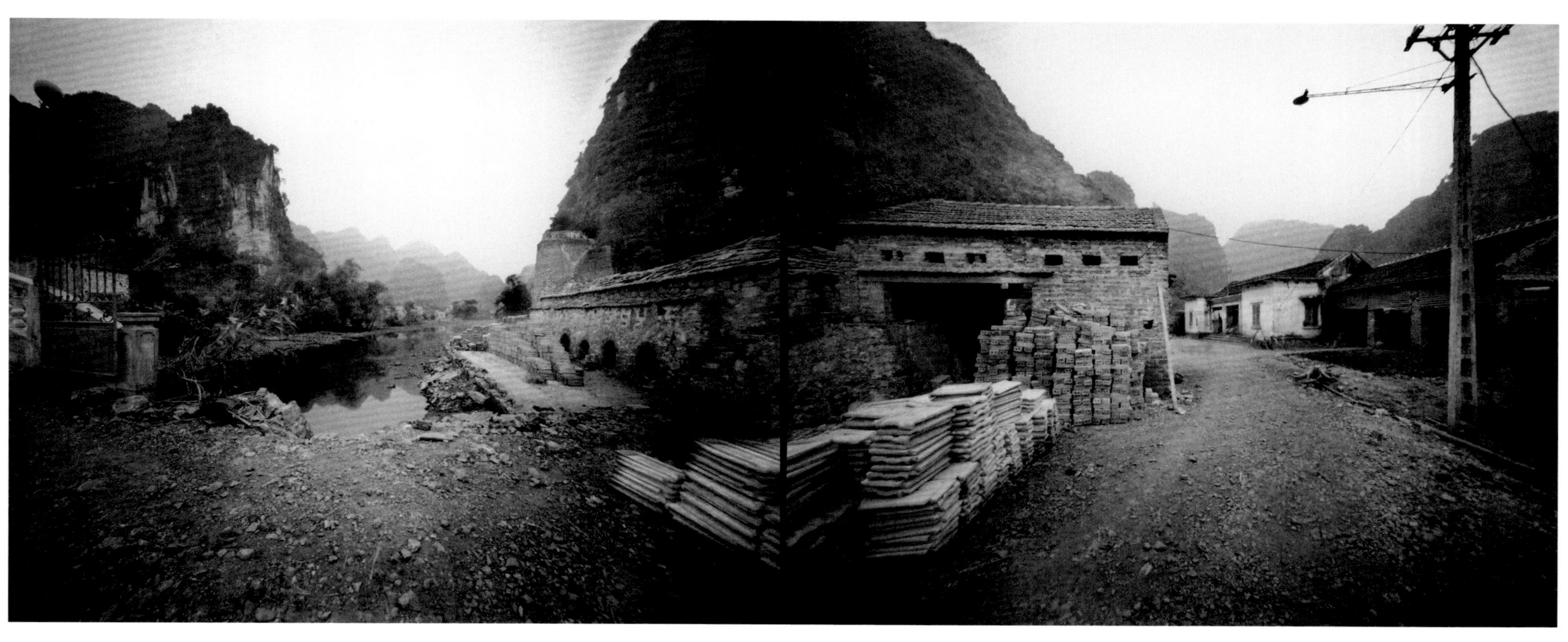

Plate 12

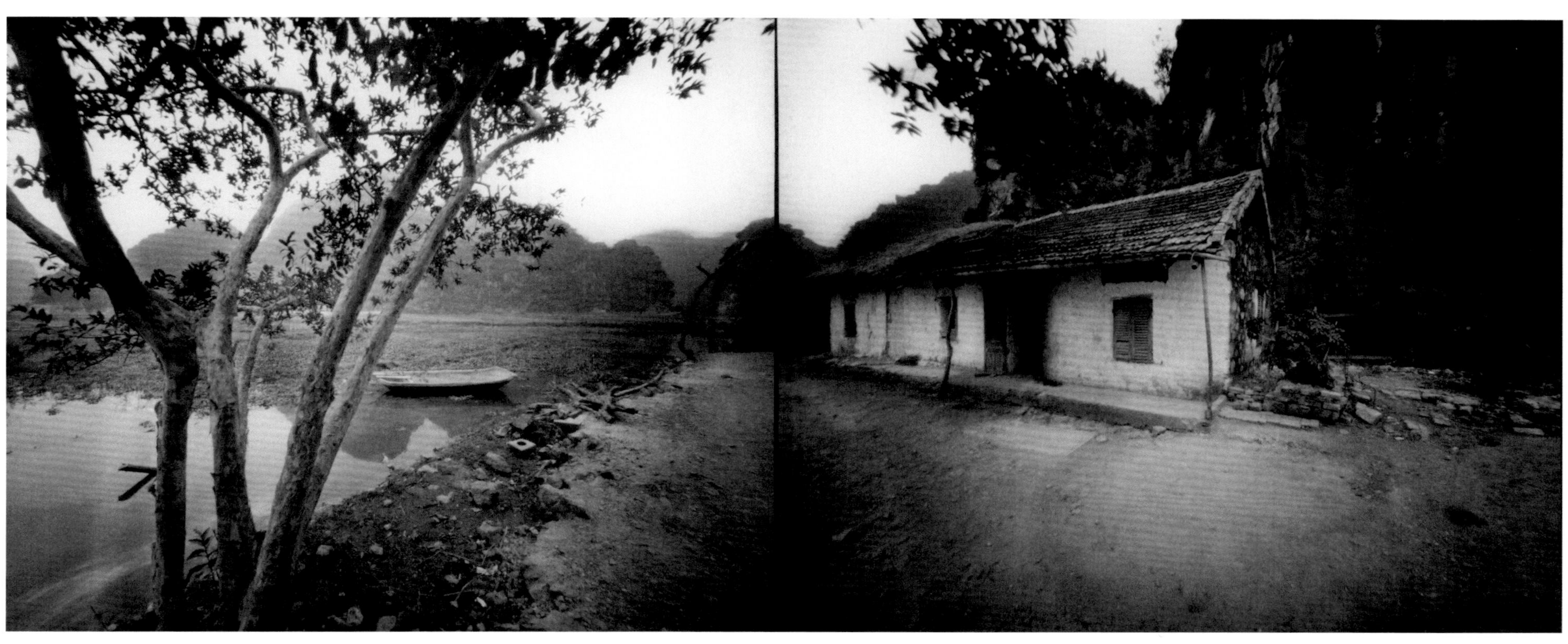

Plate 13

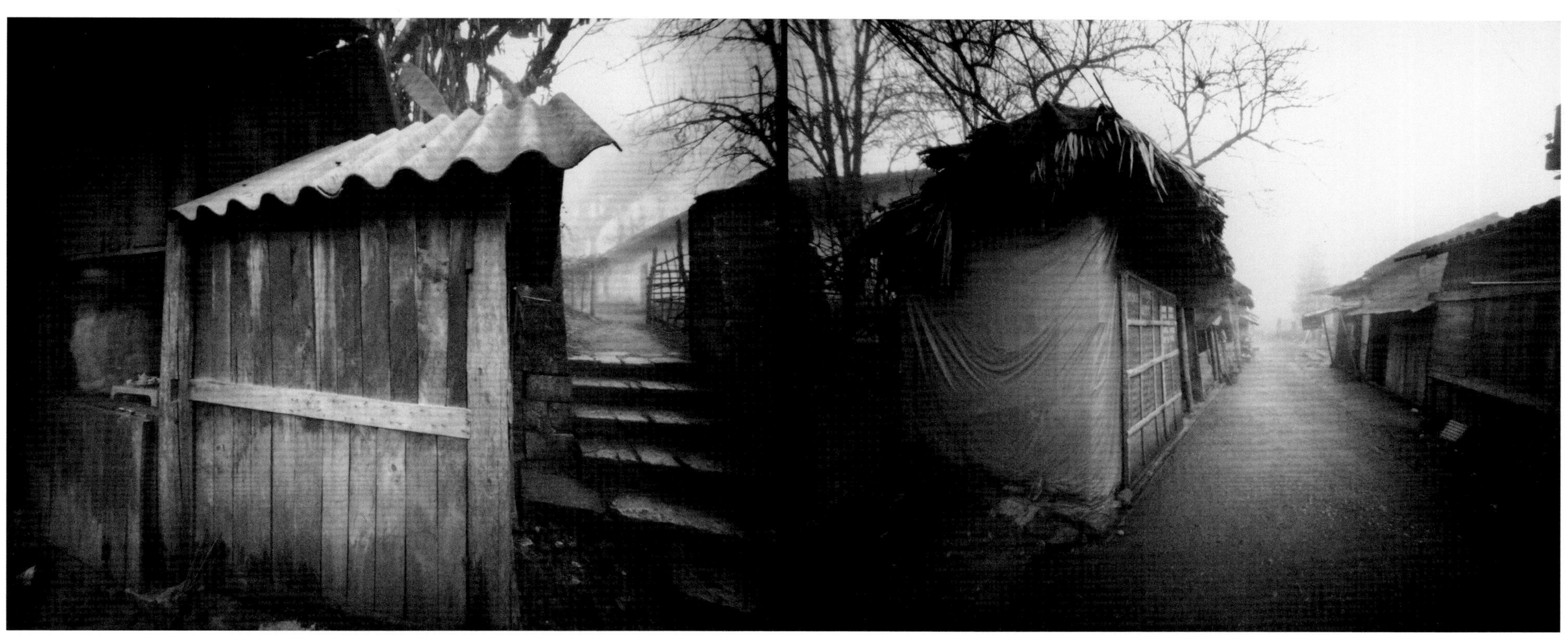

Plate 14

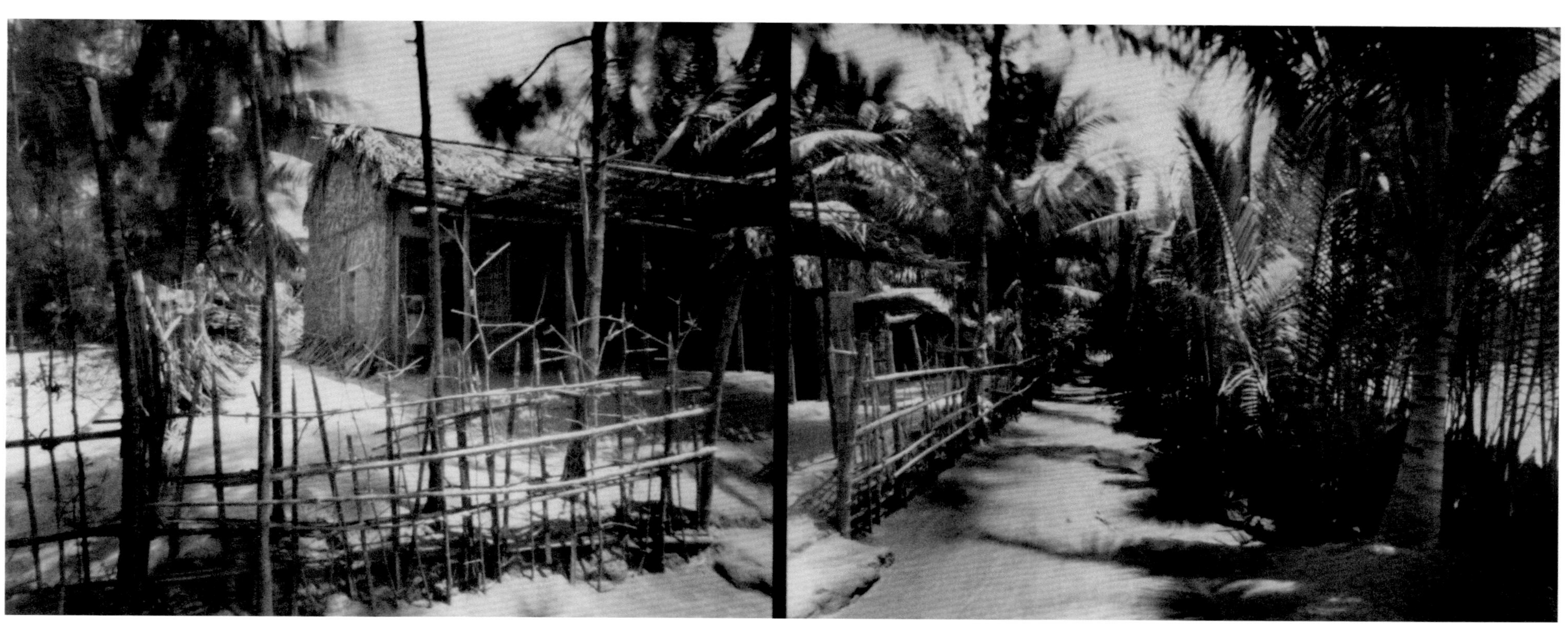

Plate 15

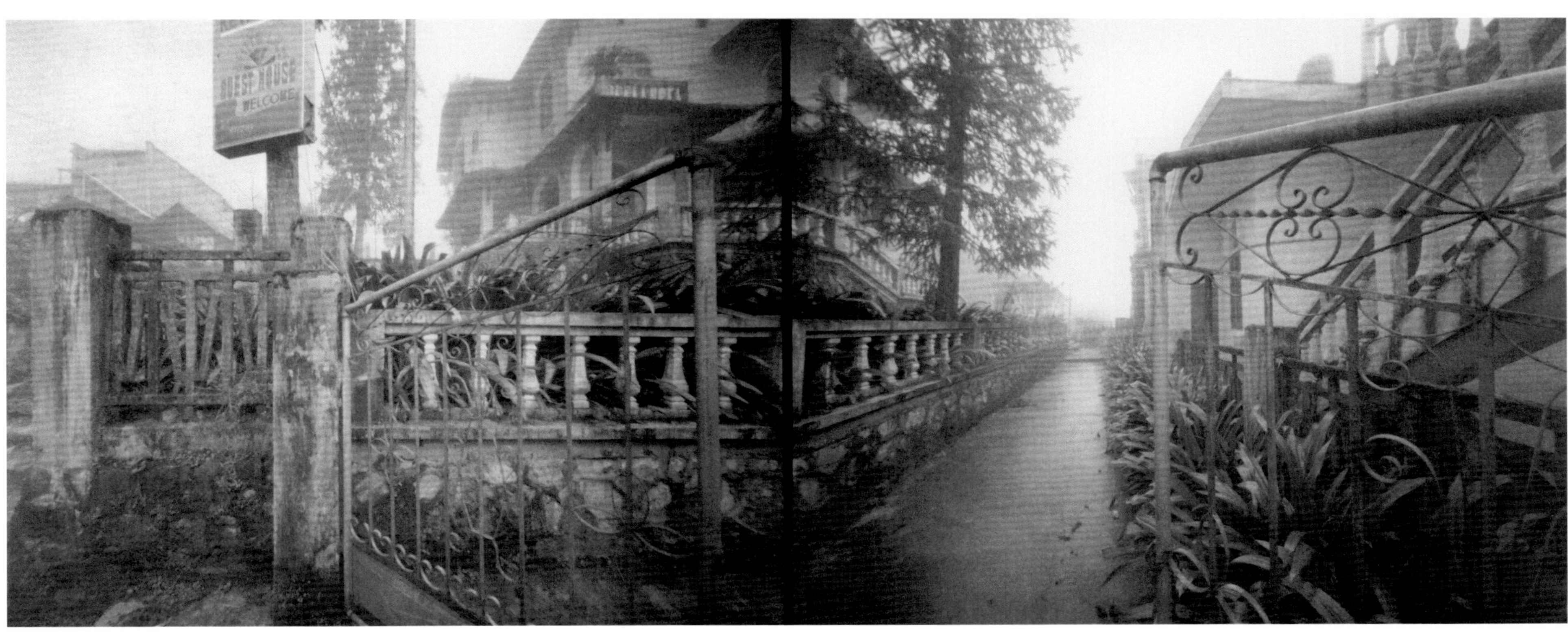
GUEST HOUSE
WELCOME

Plate 16

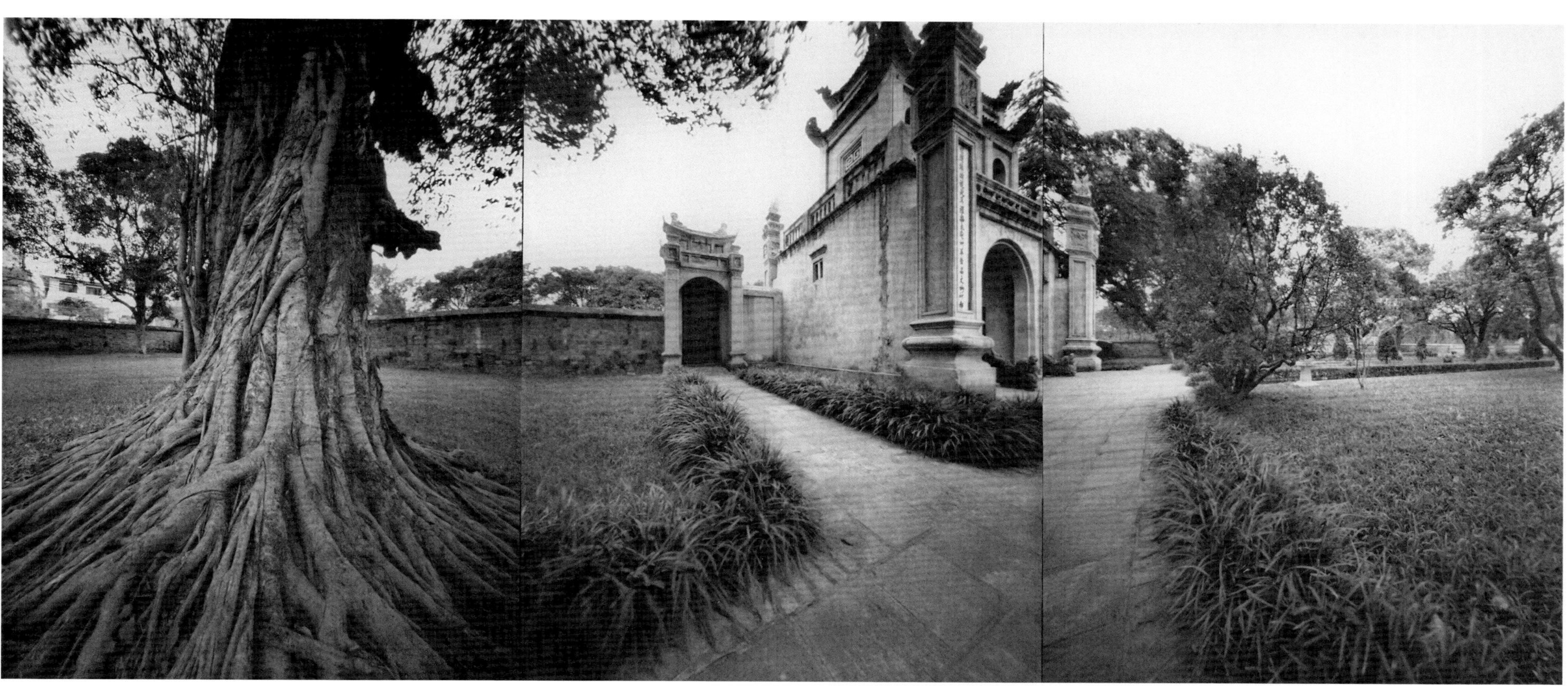

Plate 17

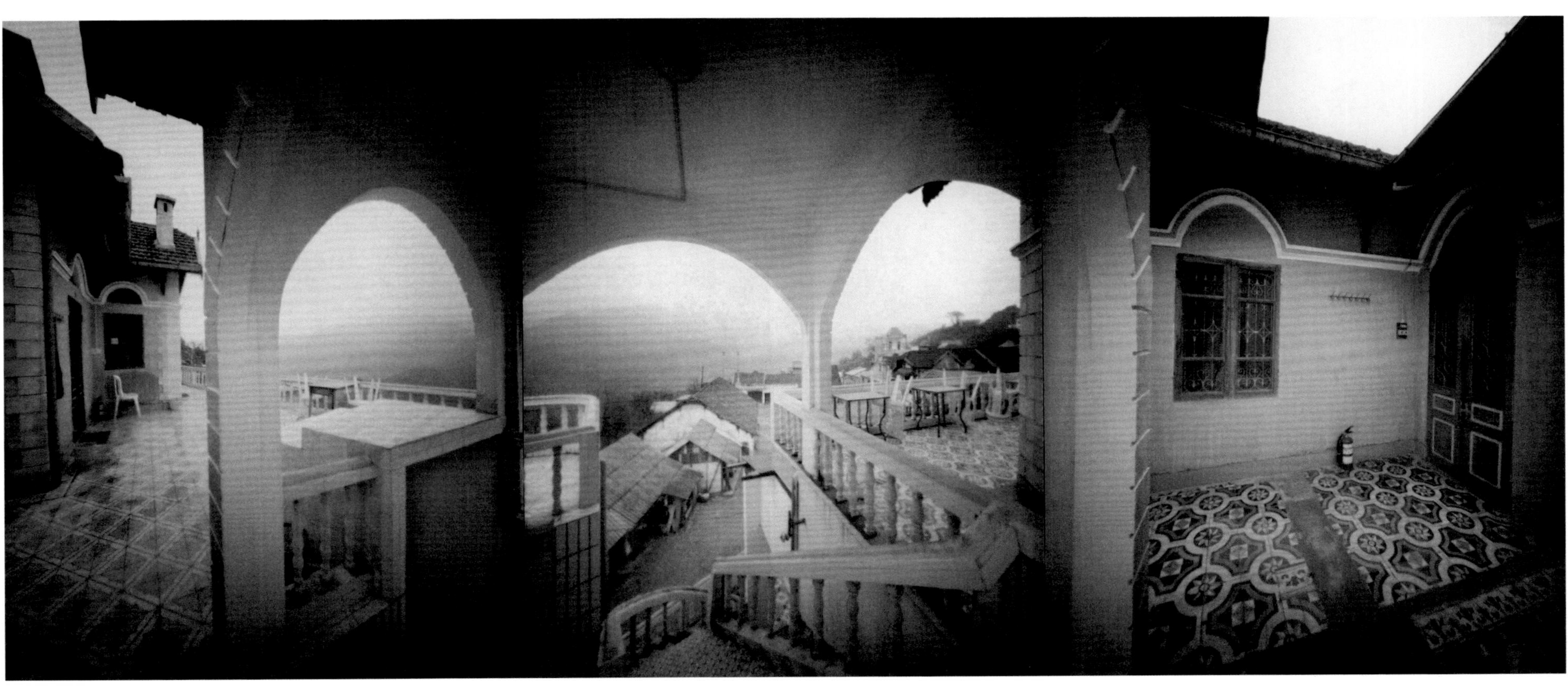

Plate 18

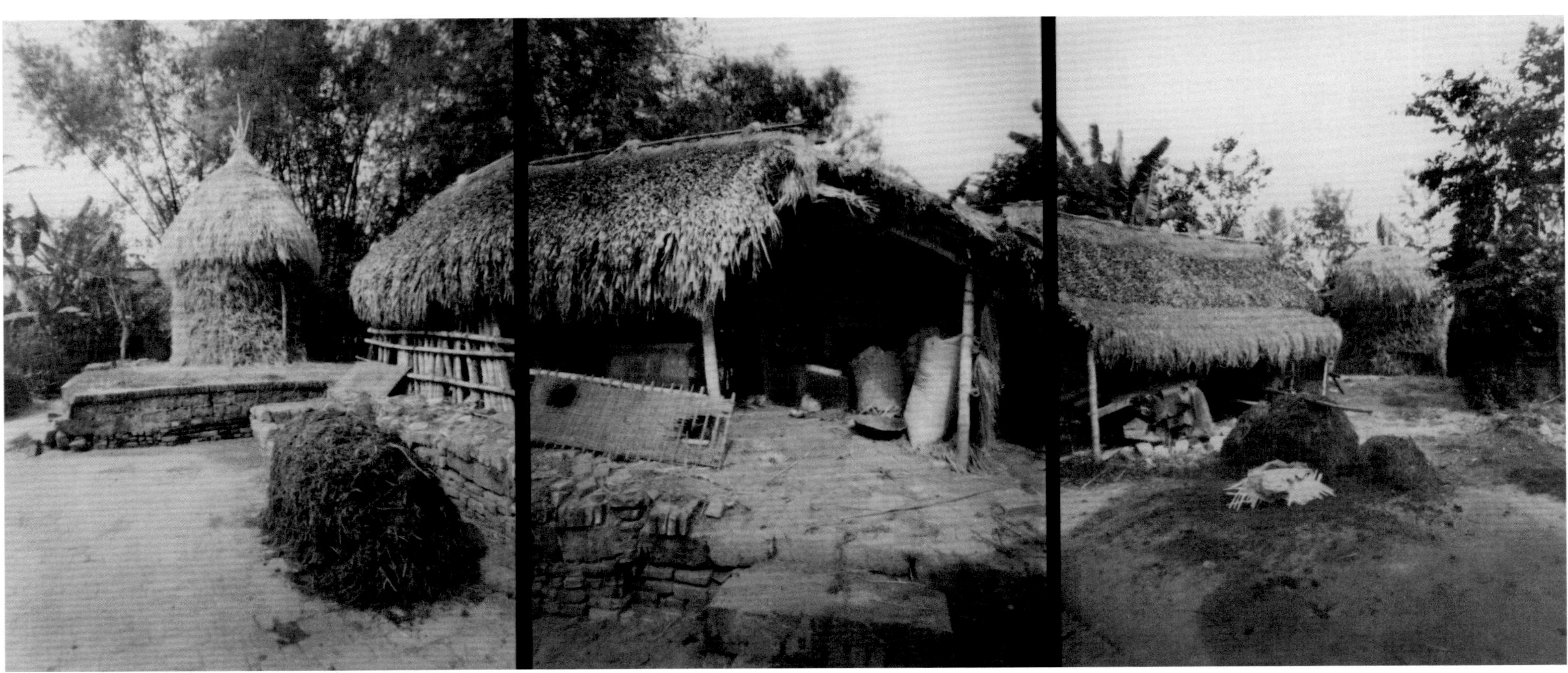

Plate 19

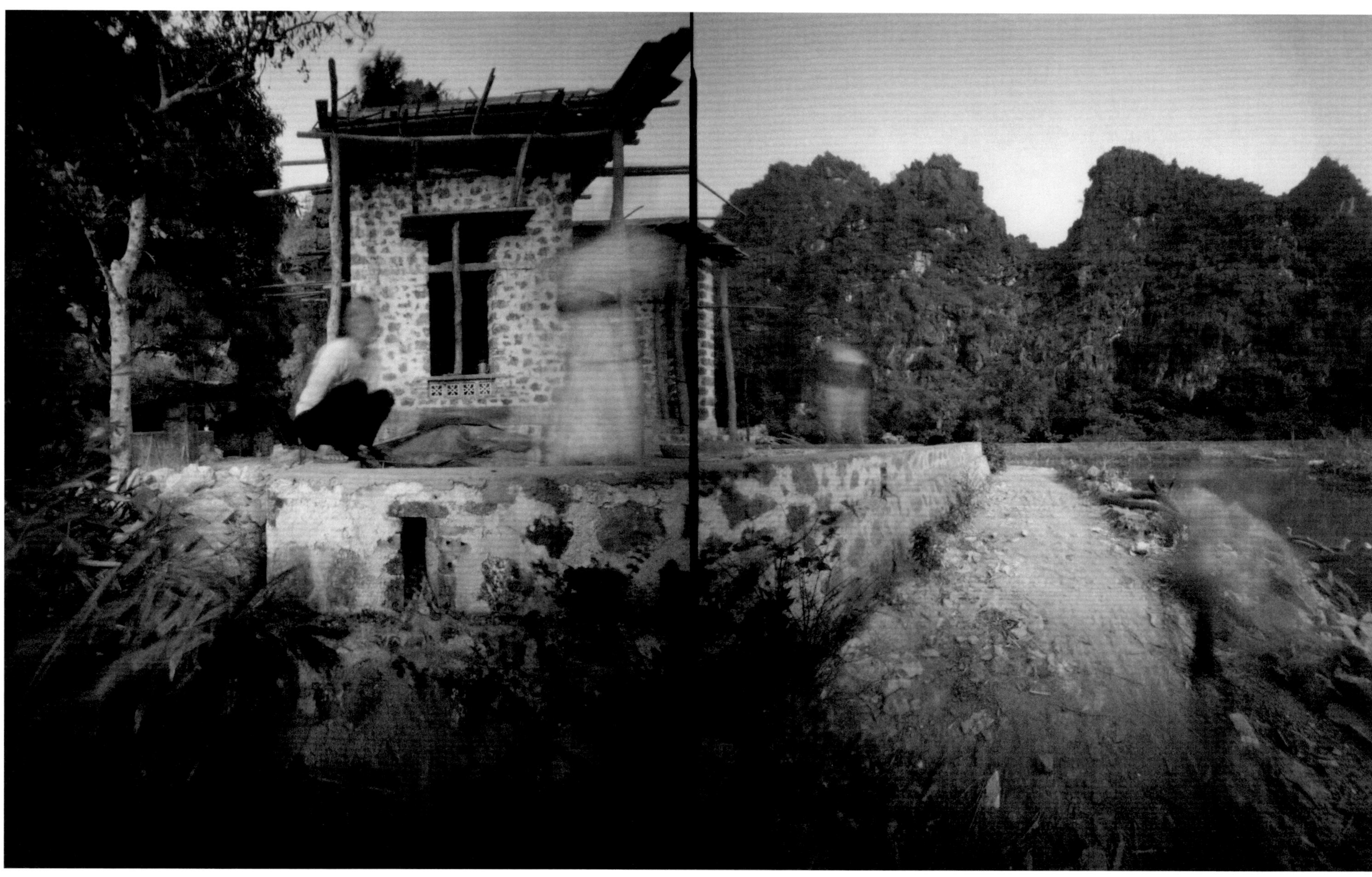

Plate 20

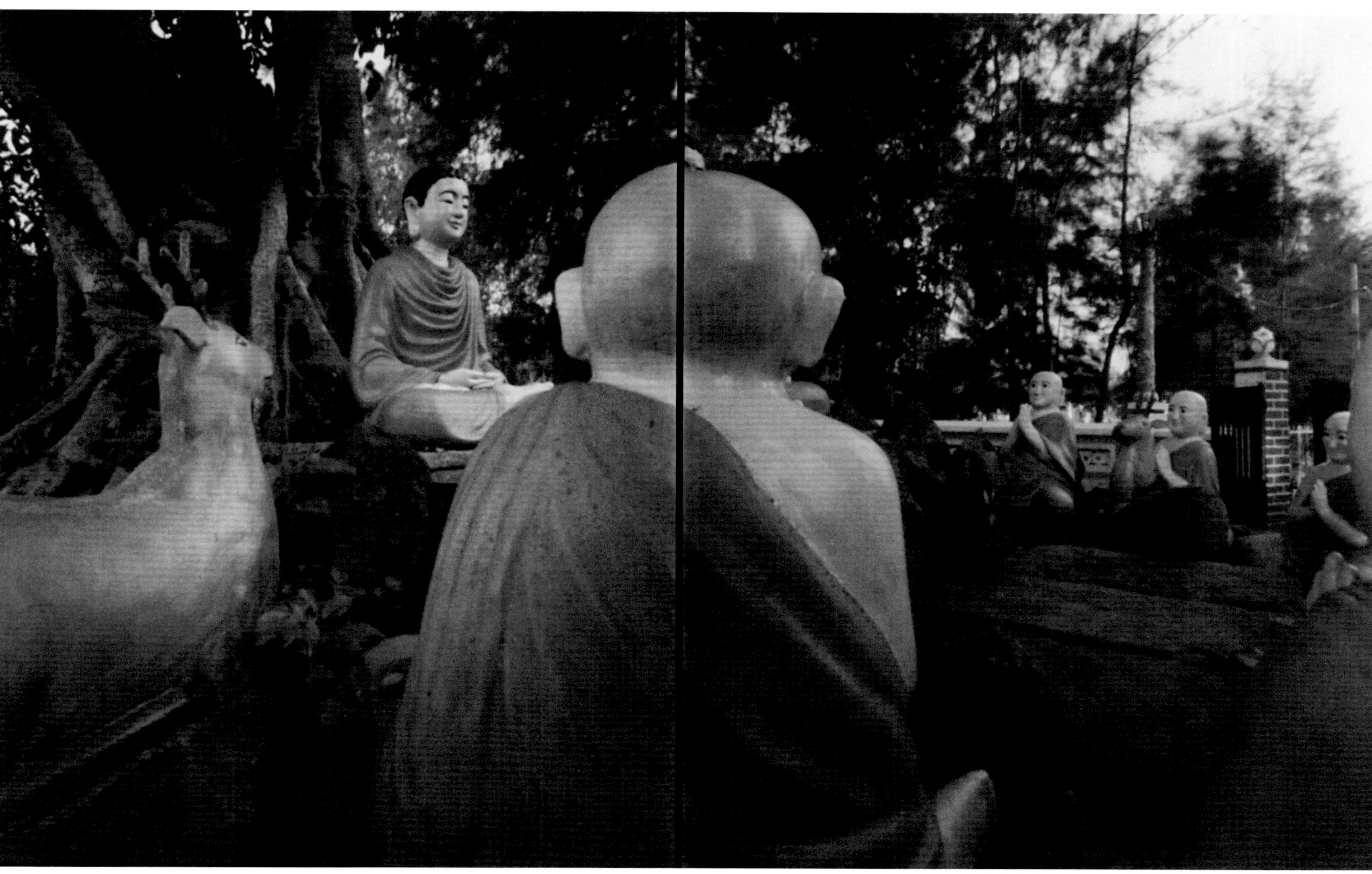

Plate 21

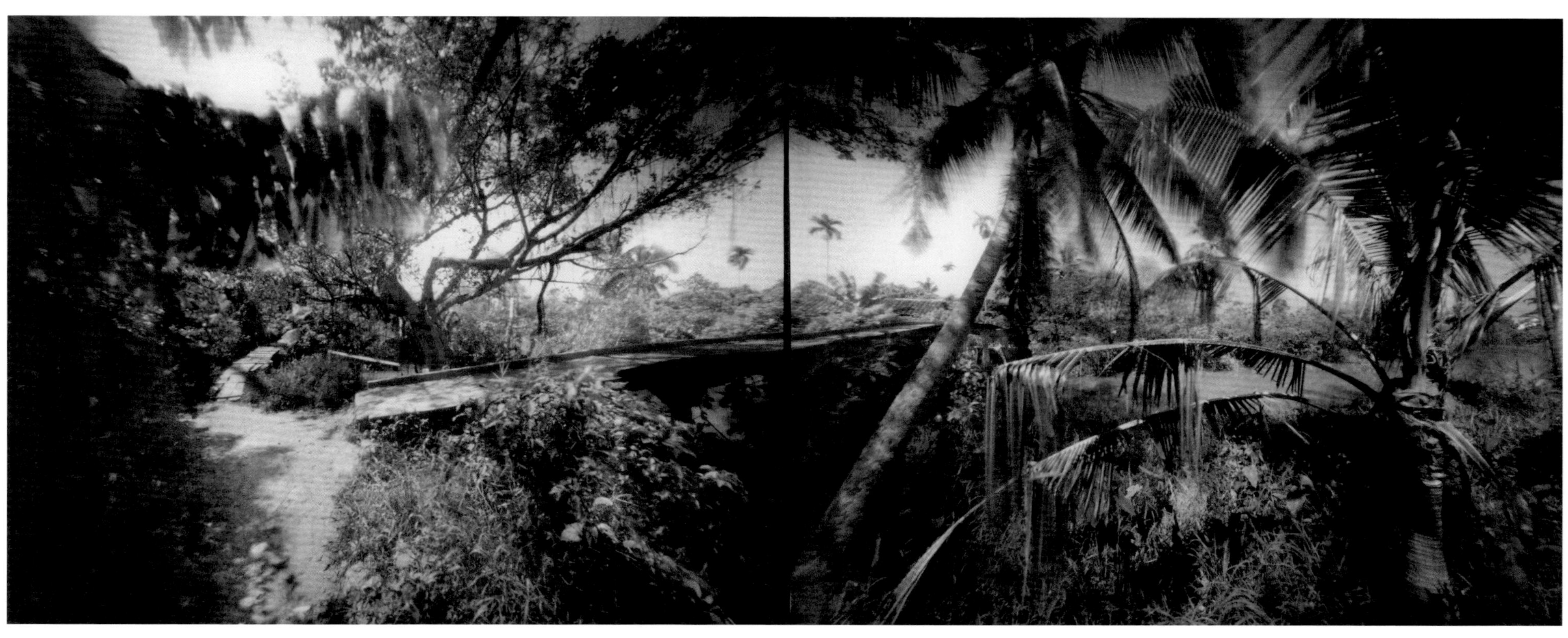

Plate 22

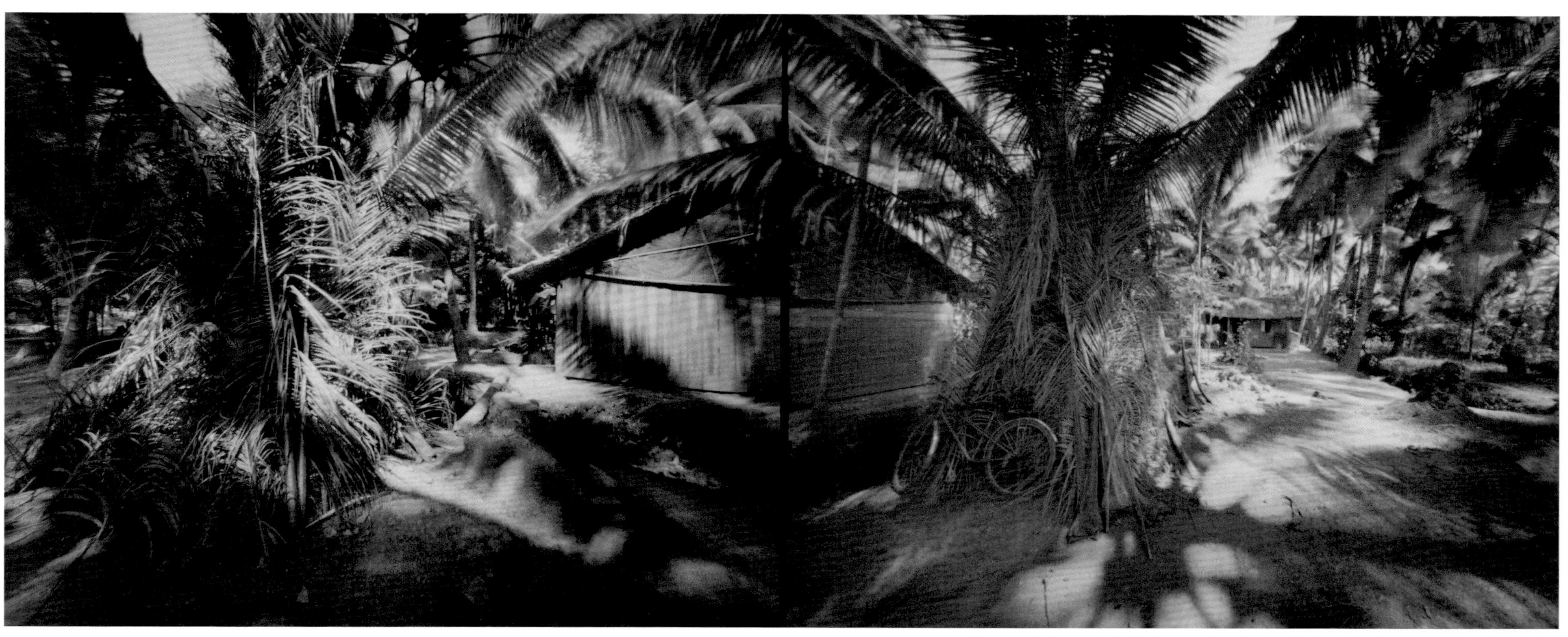

Plate 23

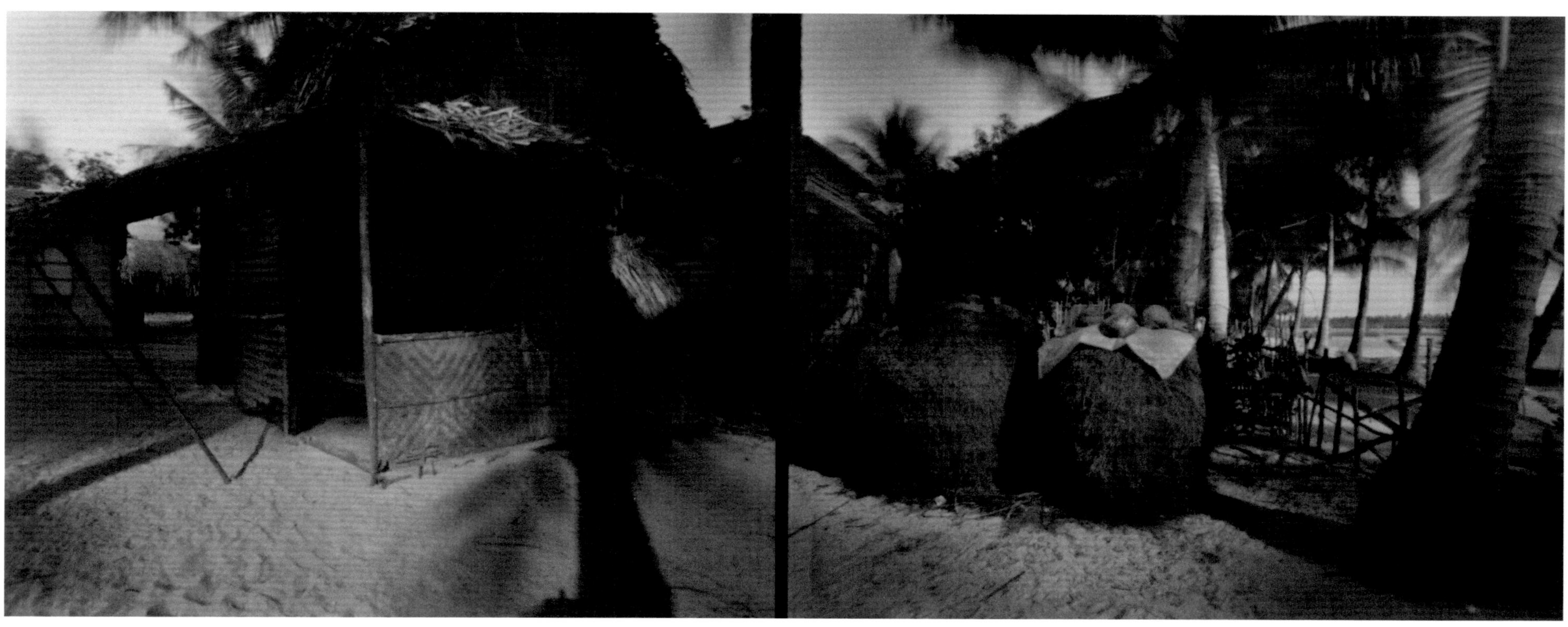

Plate 24

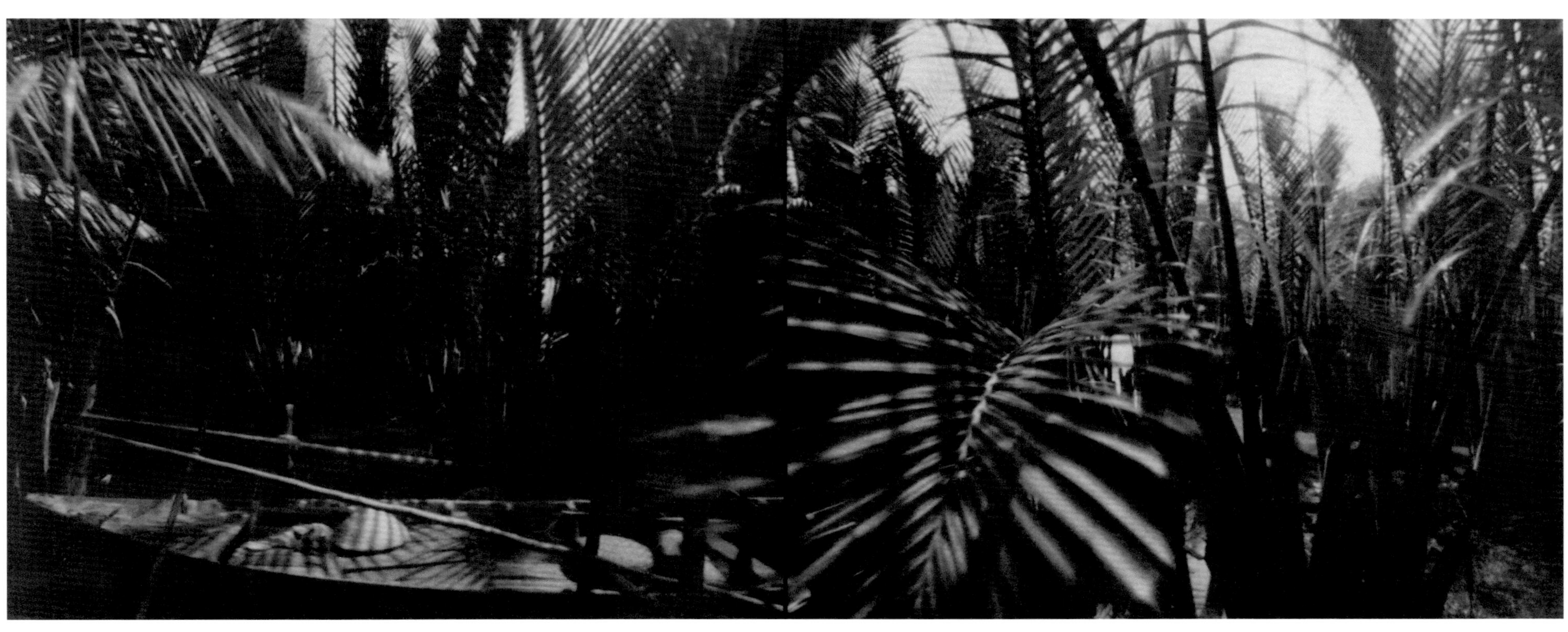

Plate 25

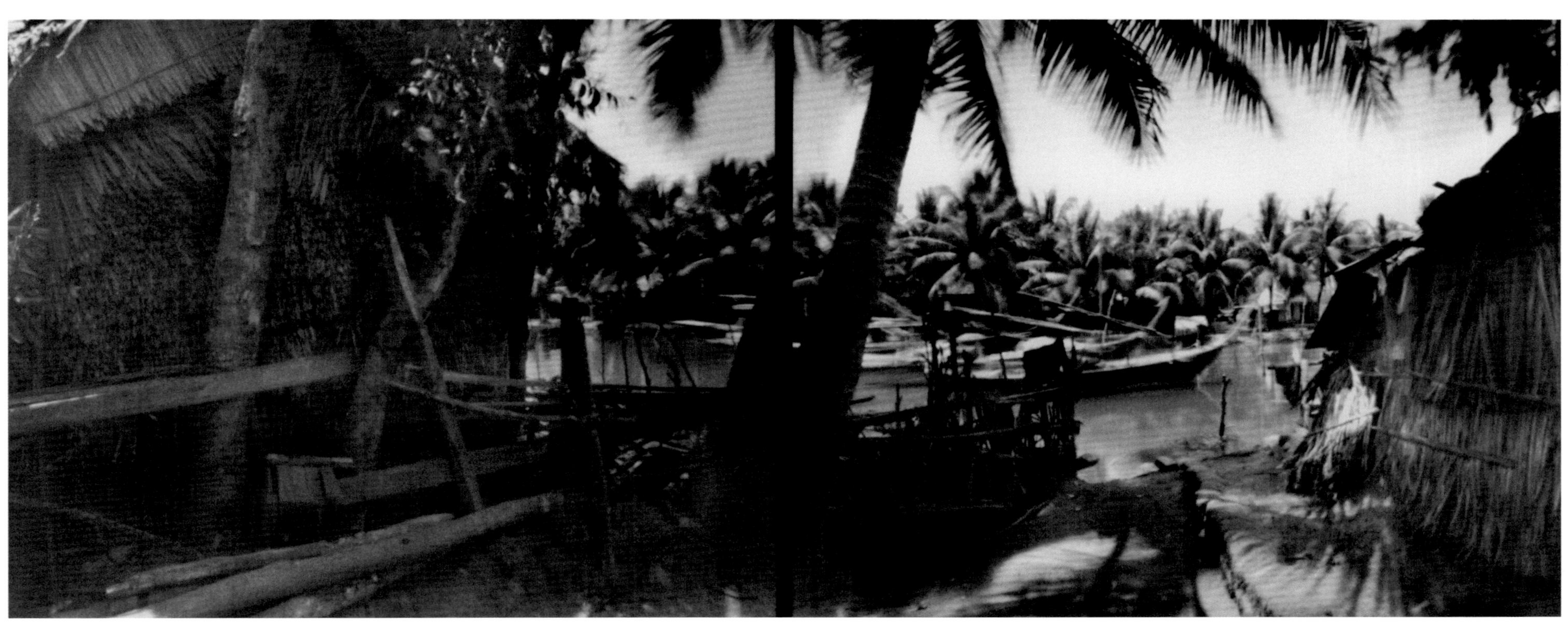

Plate 26

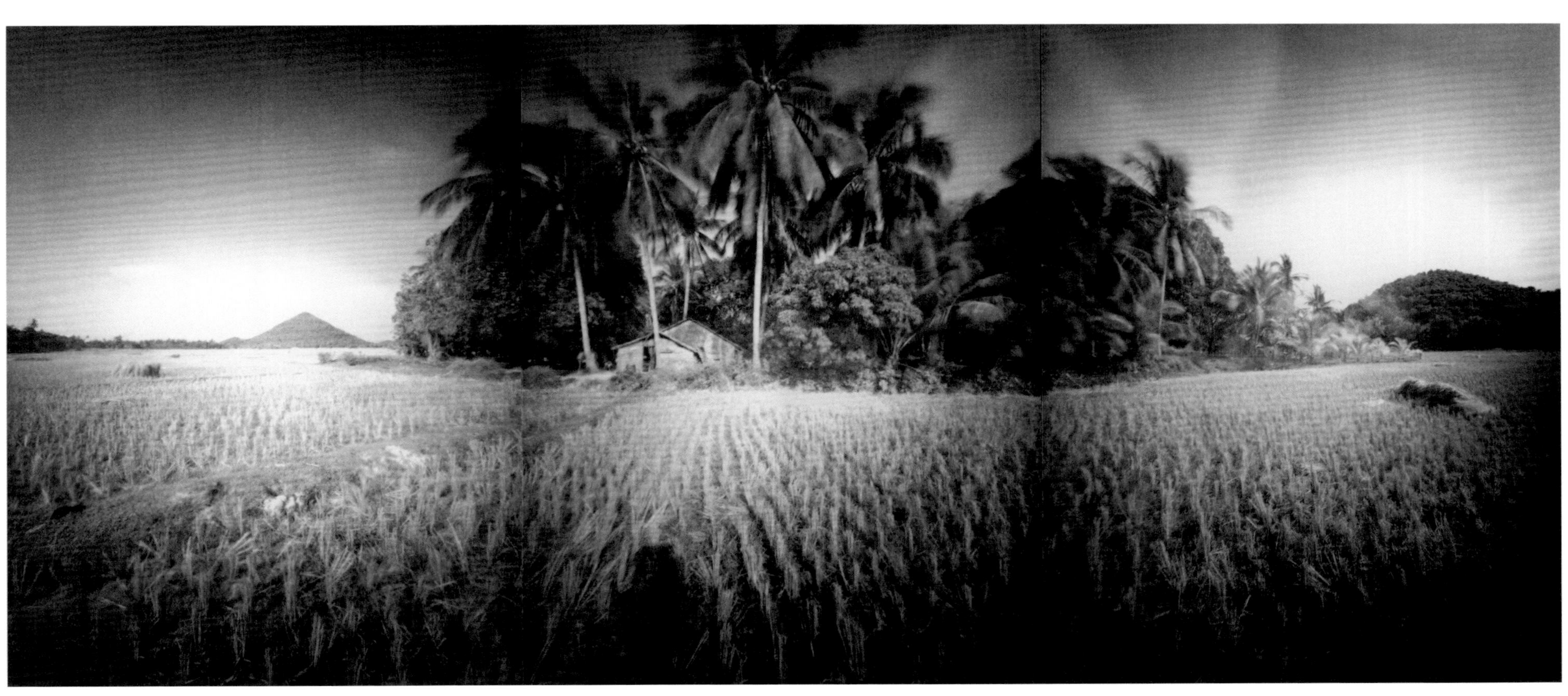

Plate 27

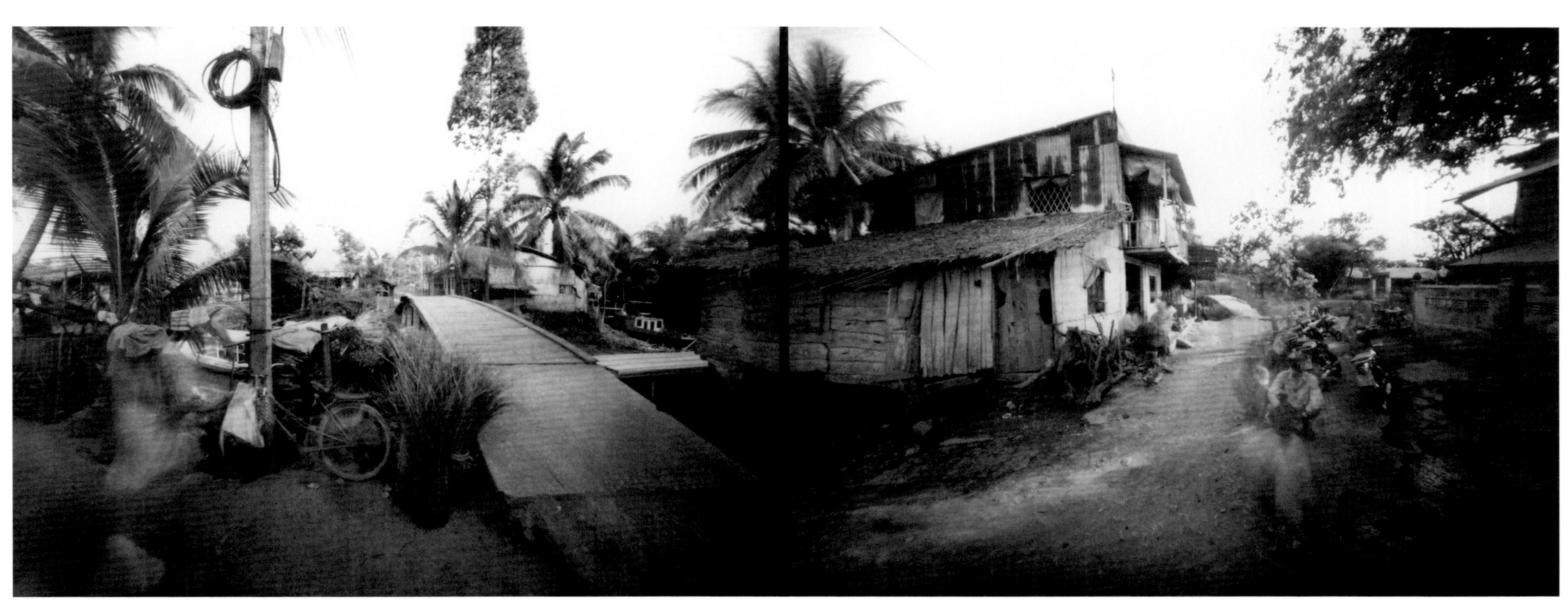

Plate 28

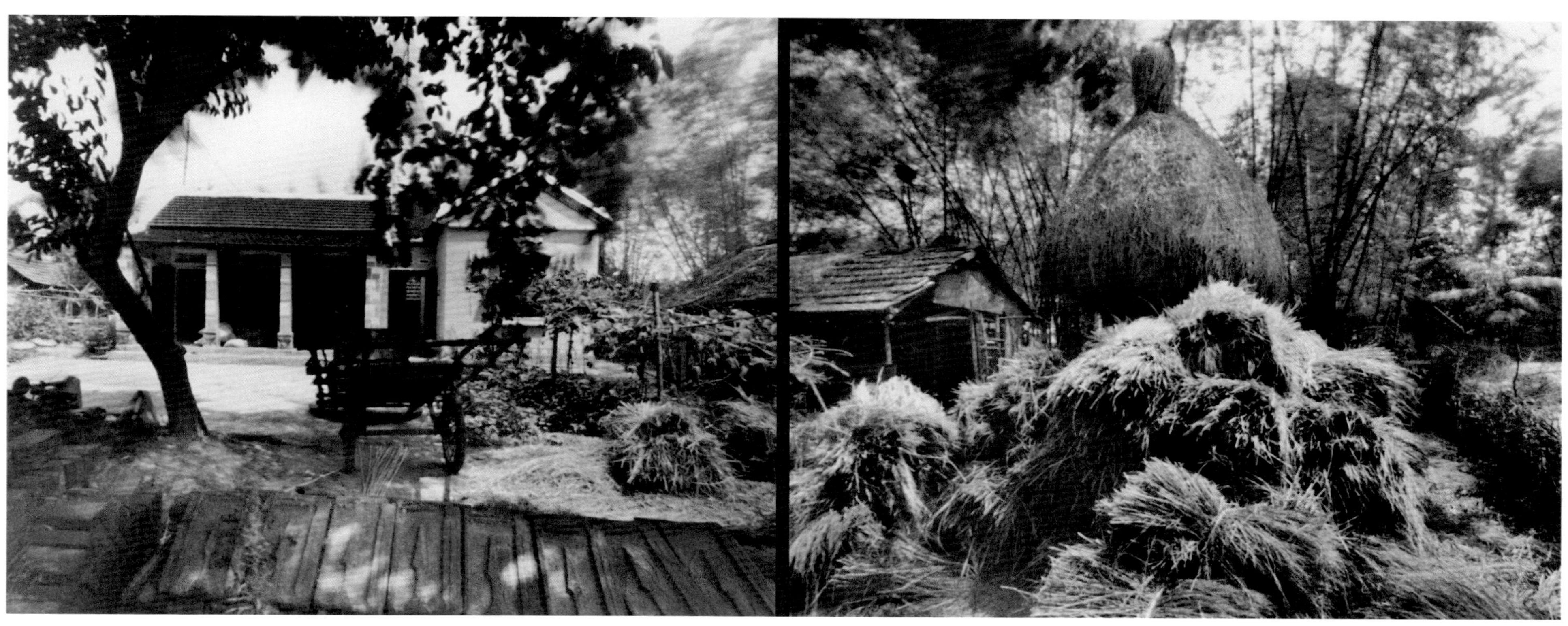

Plate 29

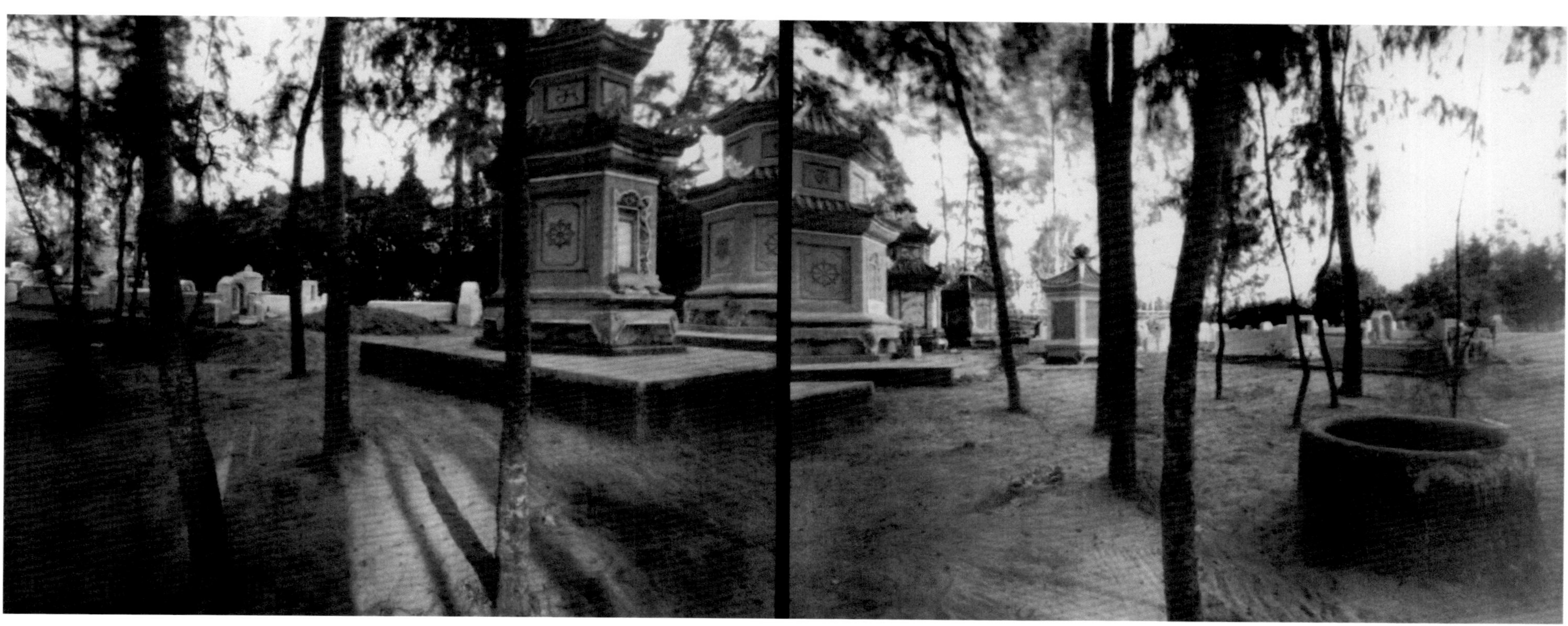

Plate 30

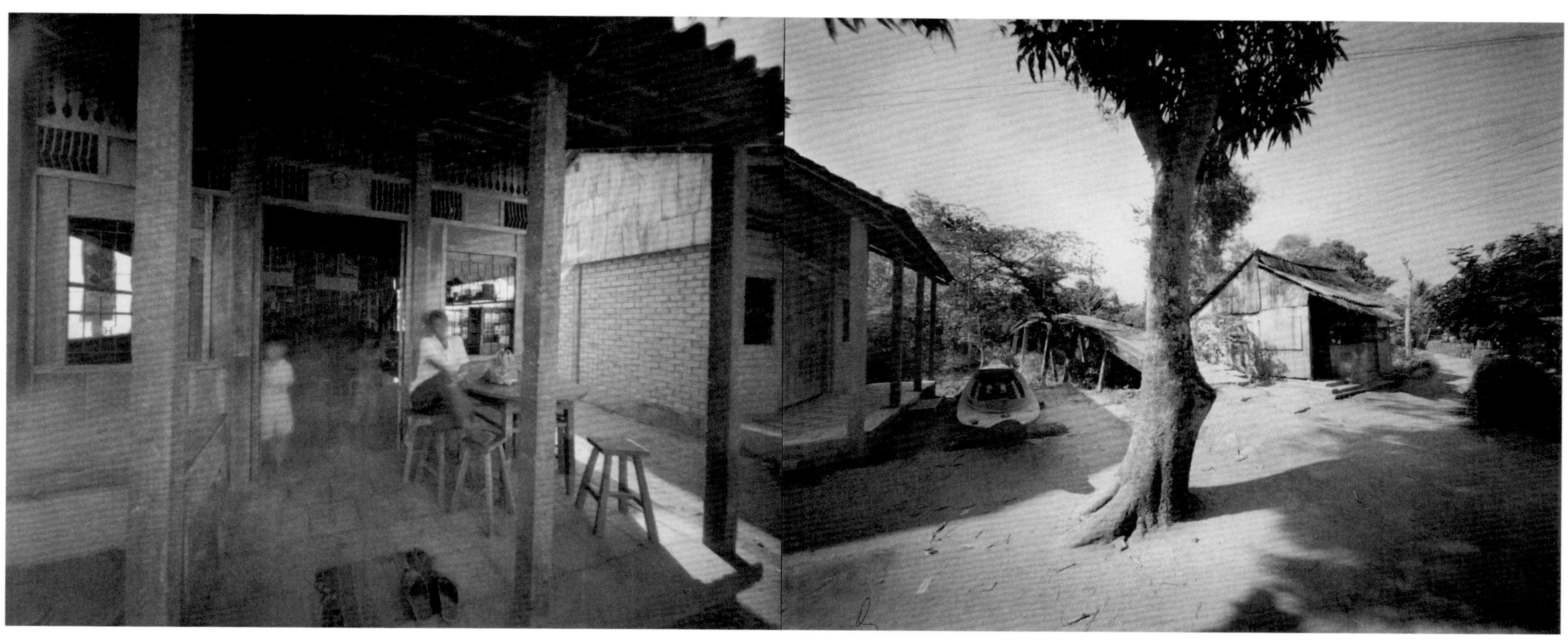

Plate 31

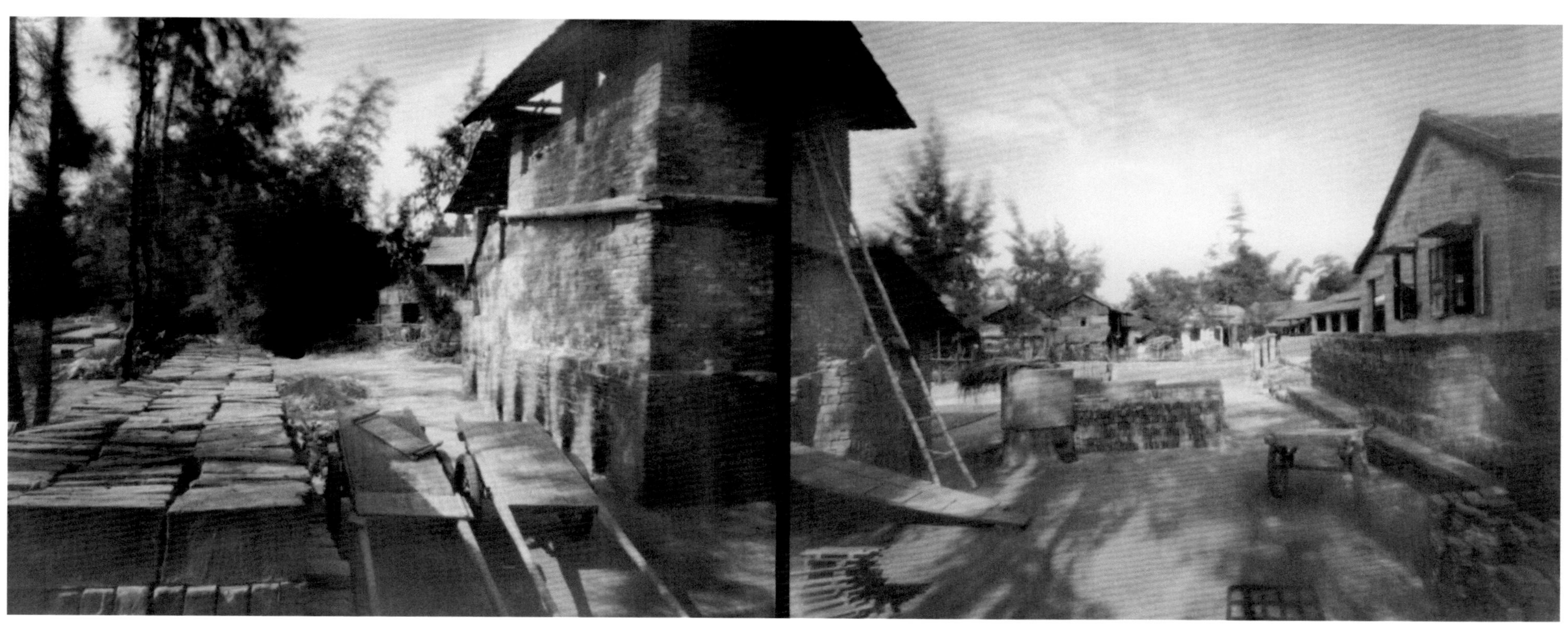

Plate 32

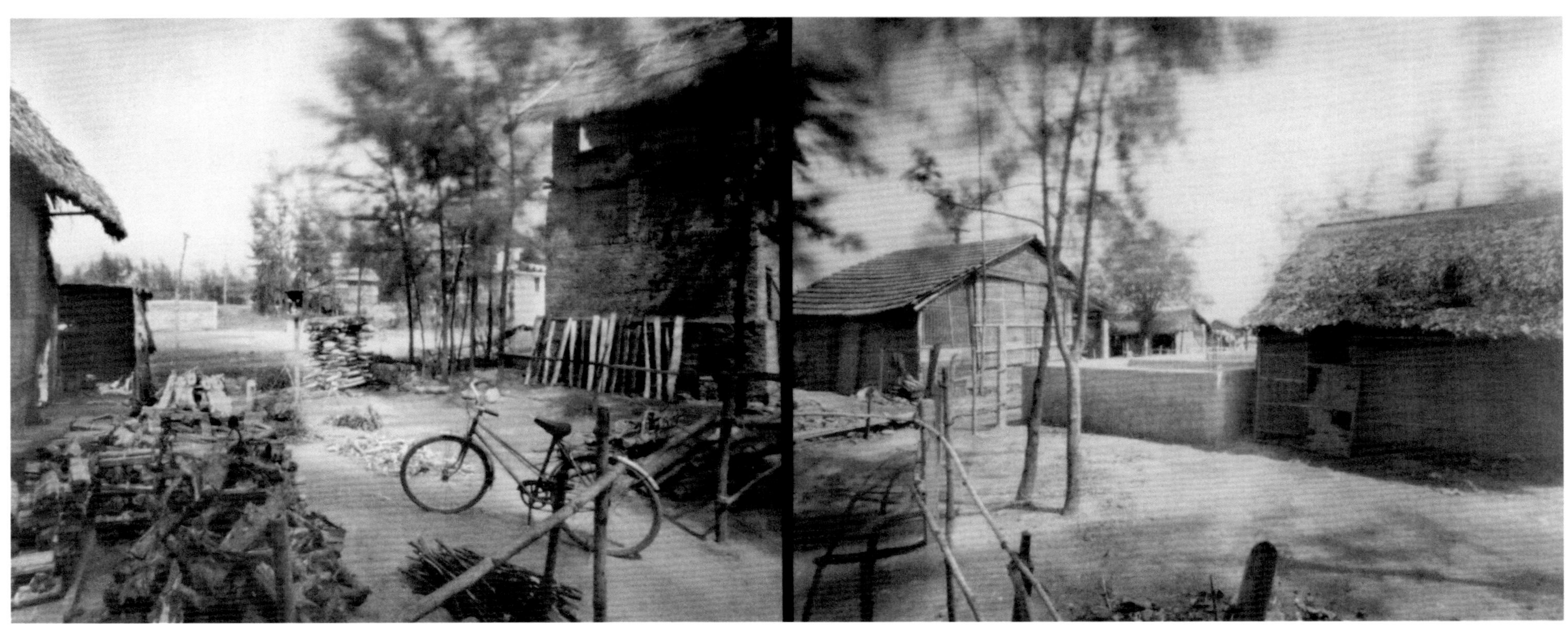

Plate 33

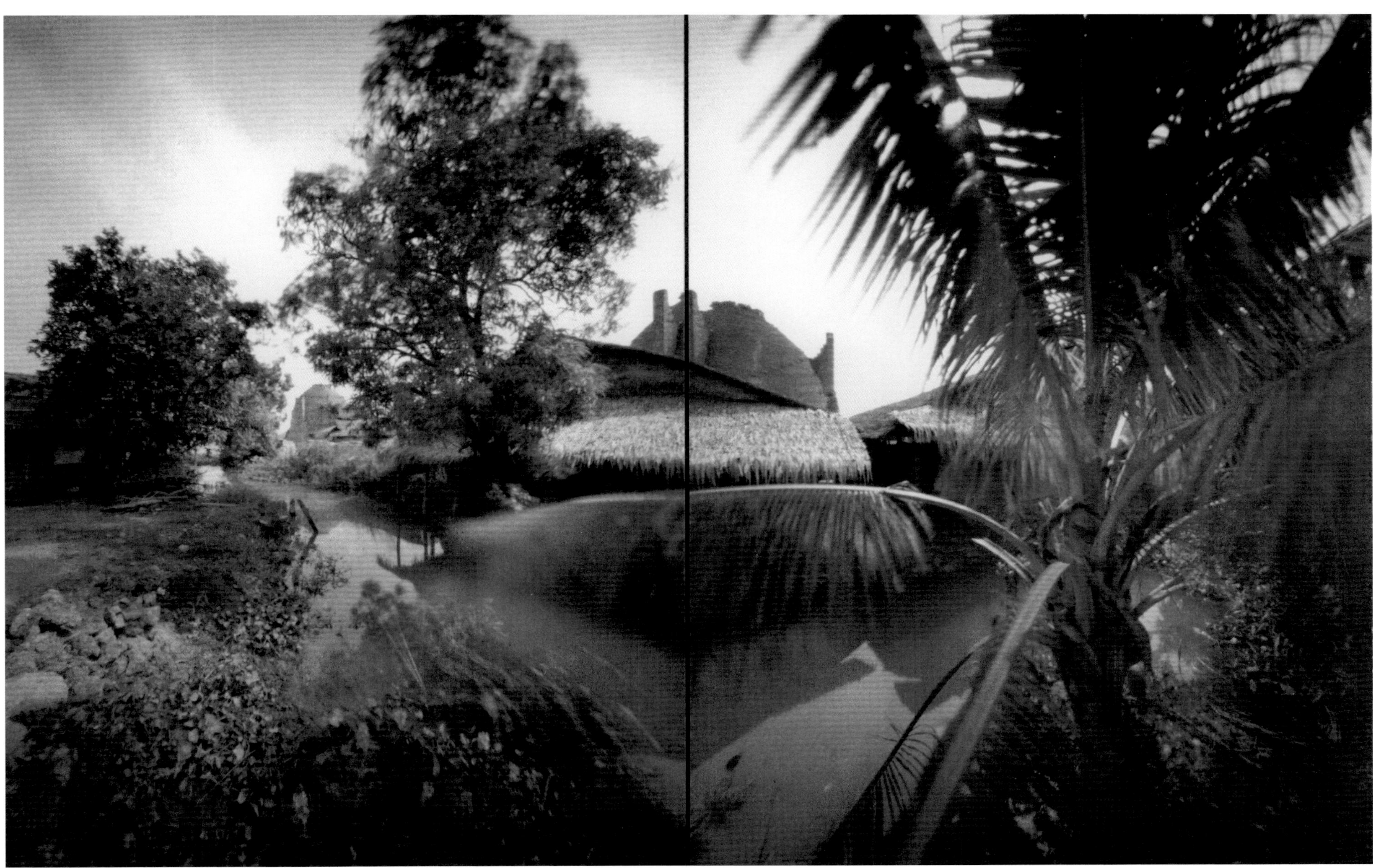

Plate 34

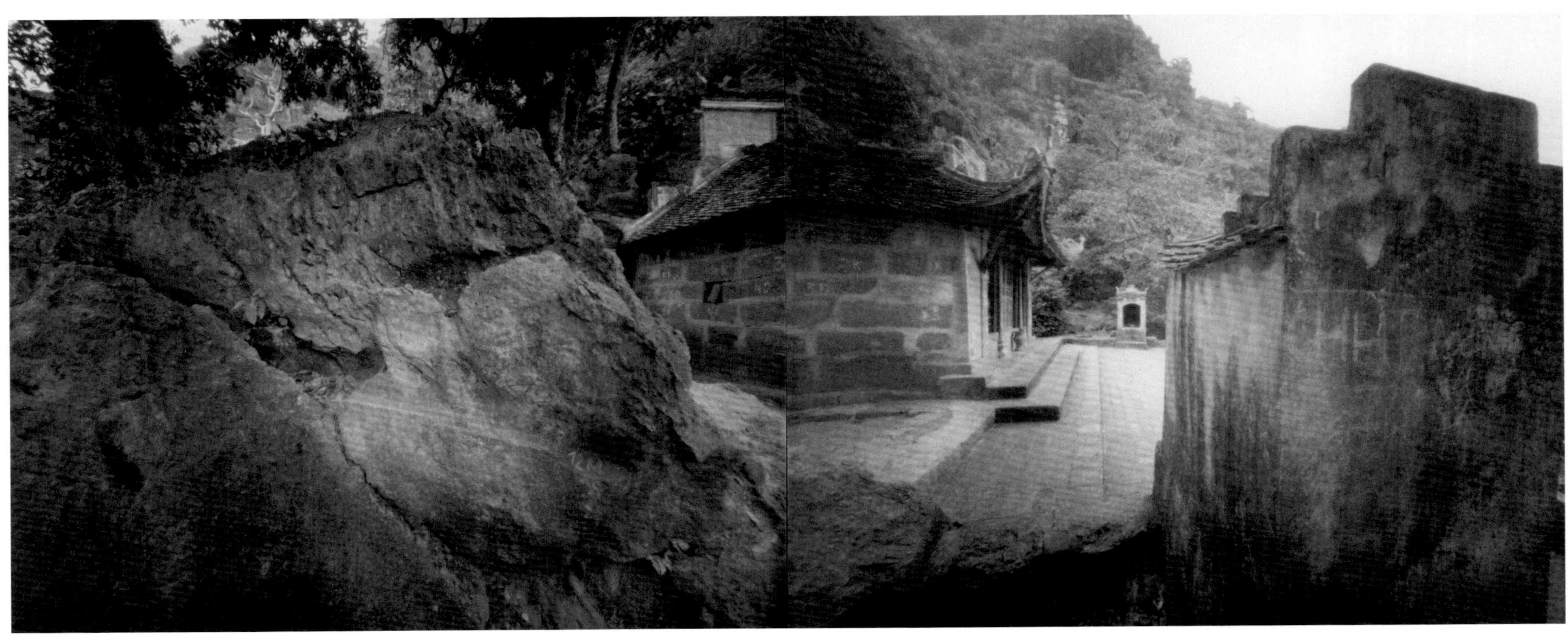

Plate 35

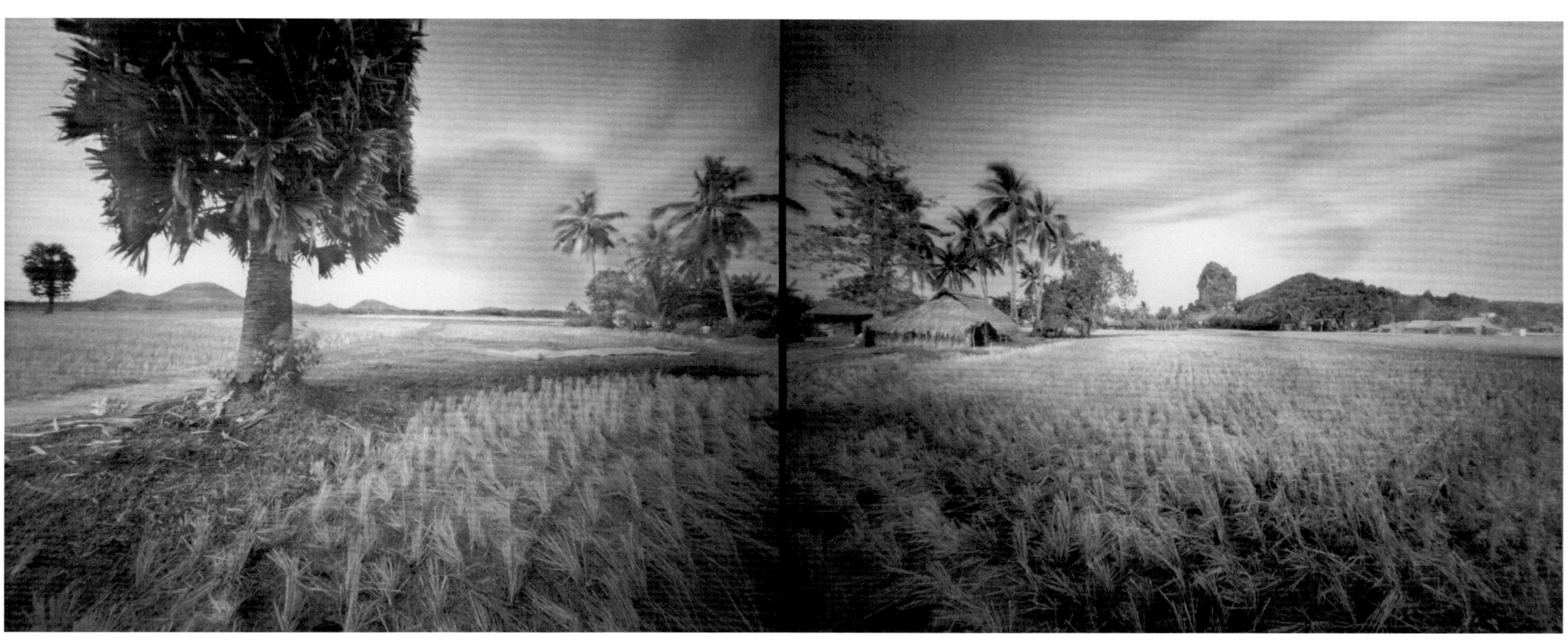

Plate 36

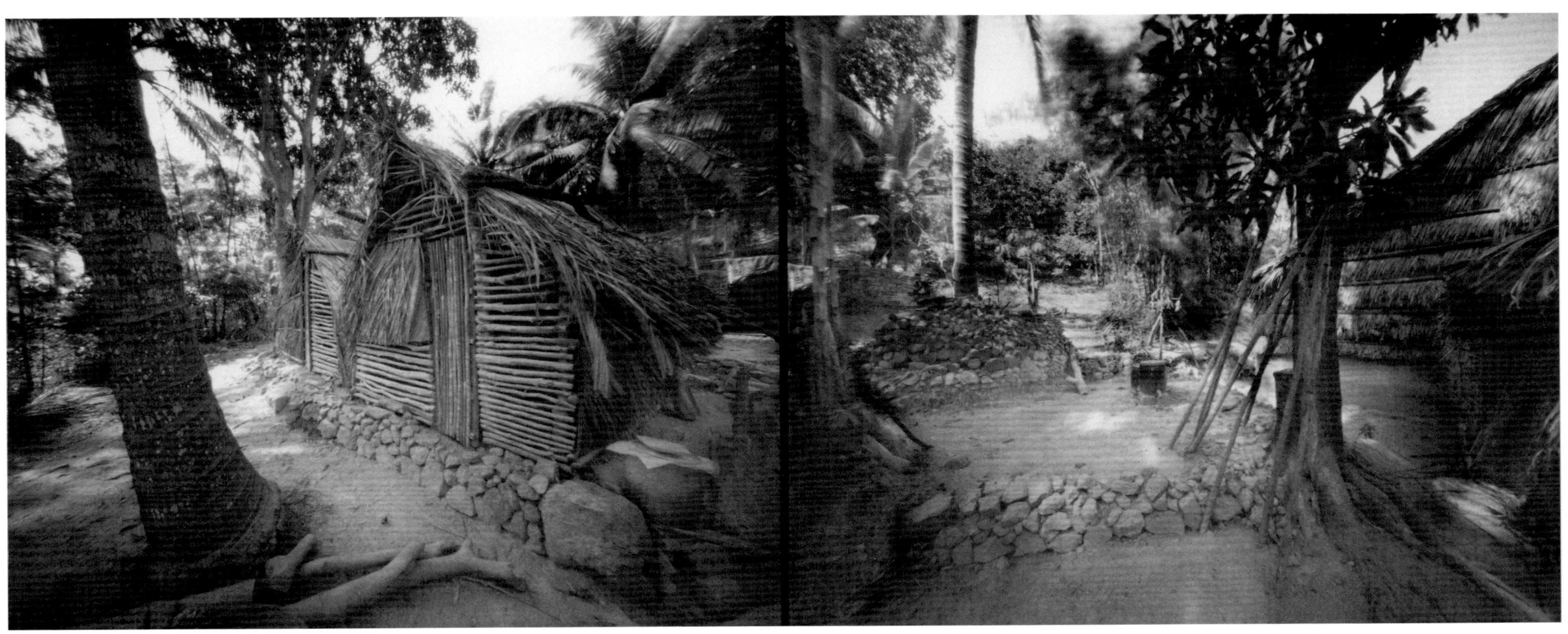

Plate 37

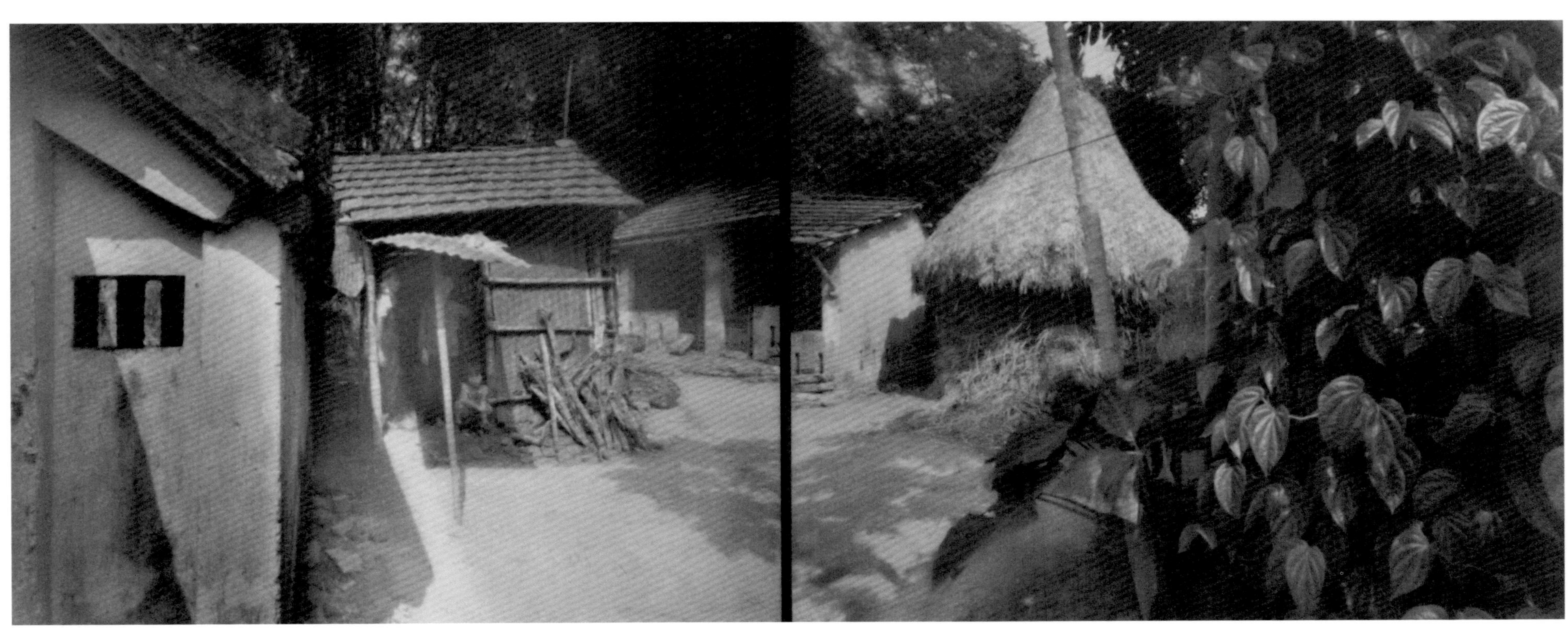

Plate 38

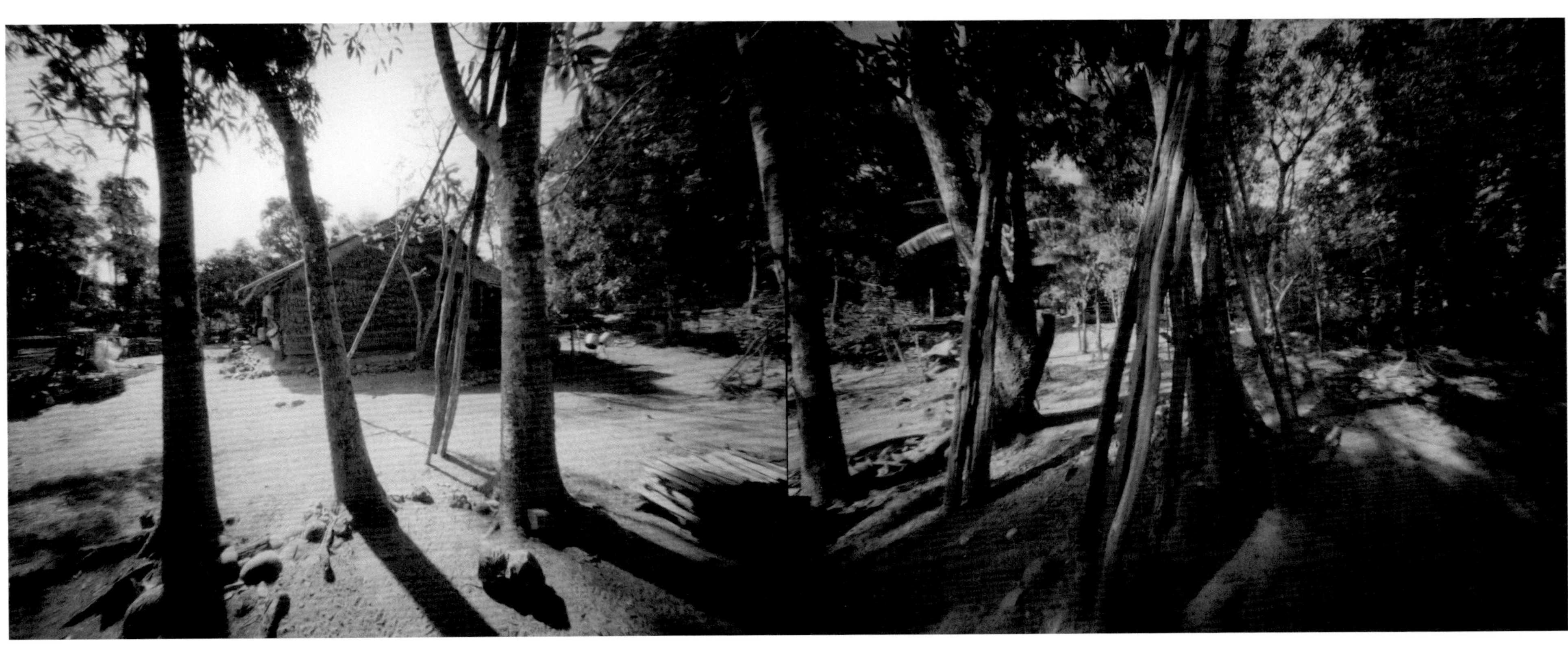

Plate 39

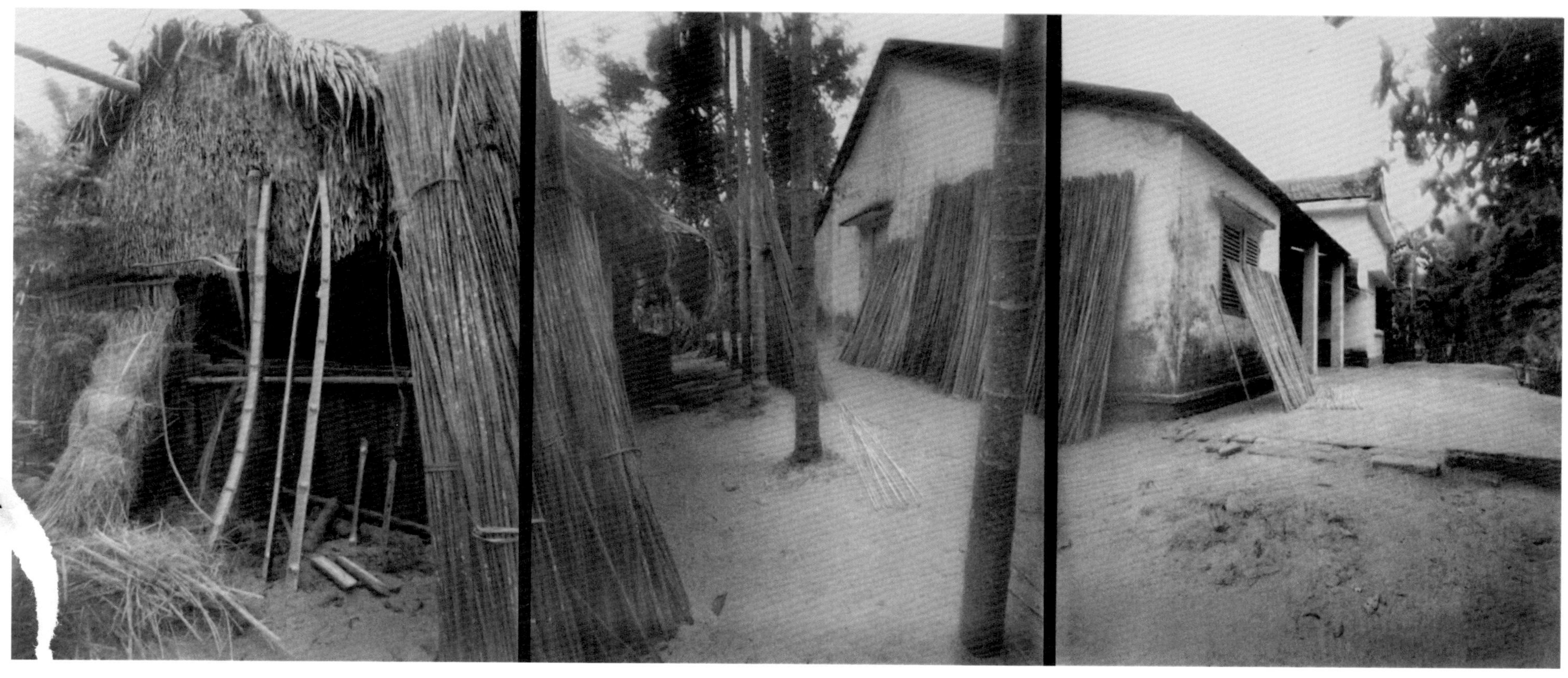

Plate 41

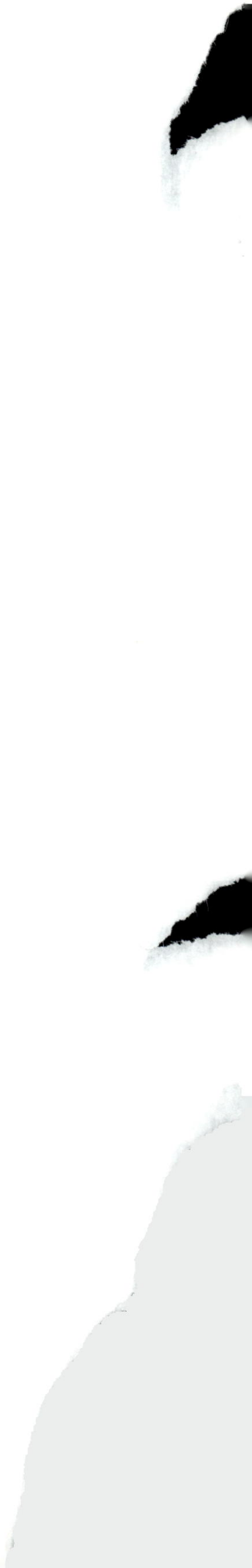

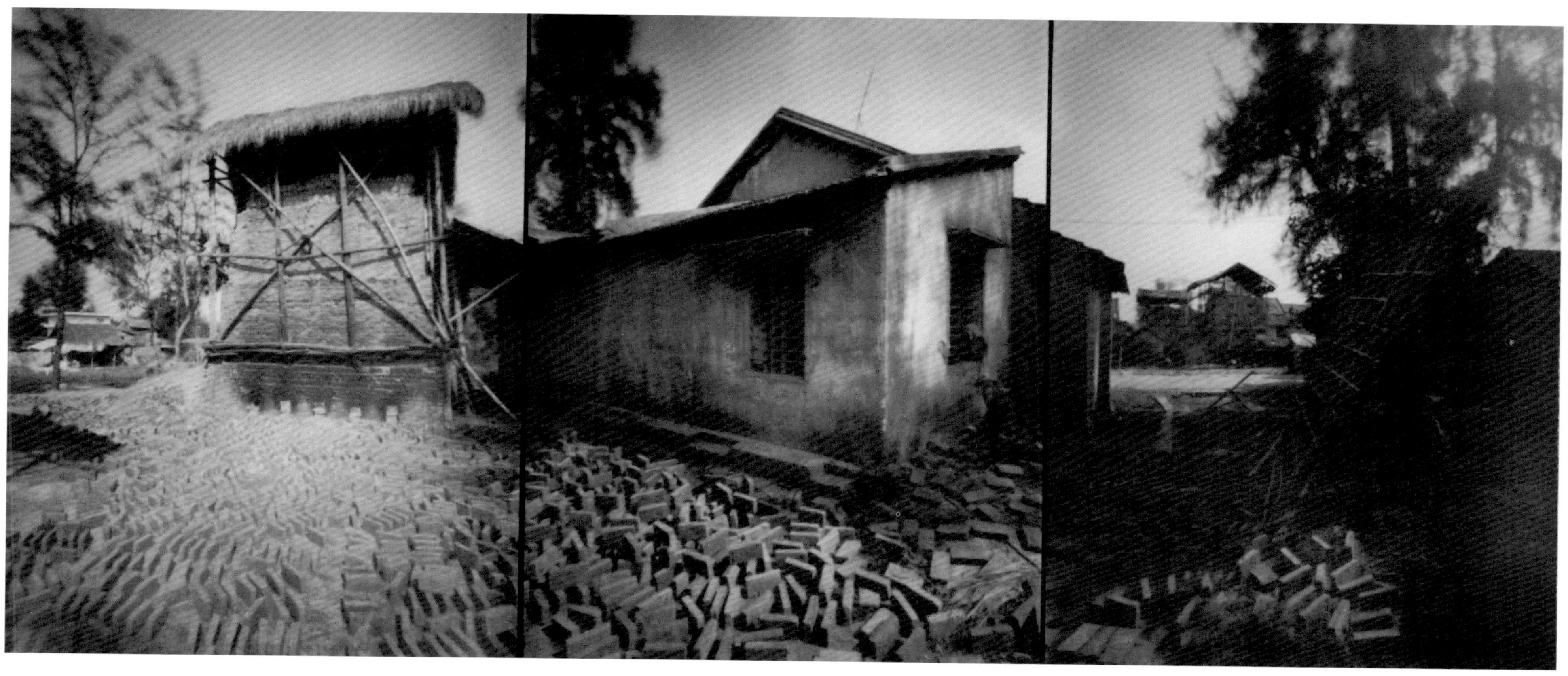

Plate 42

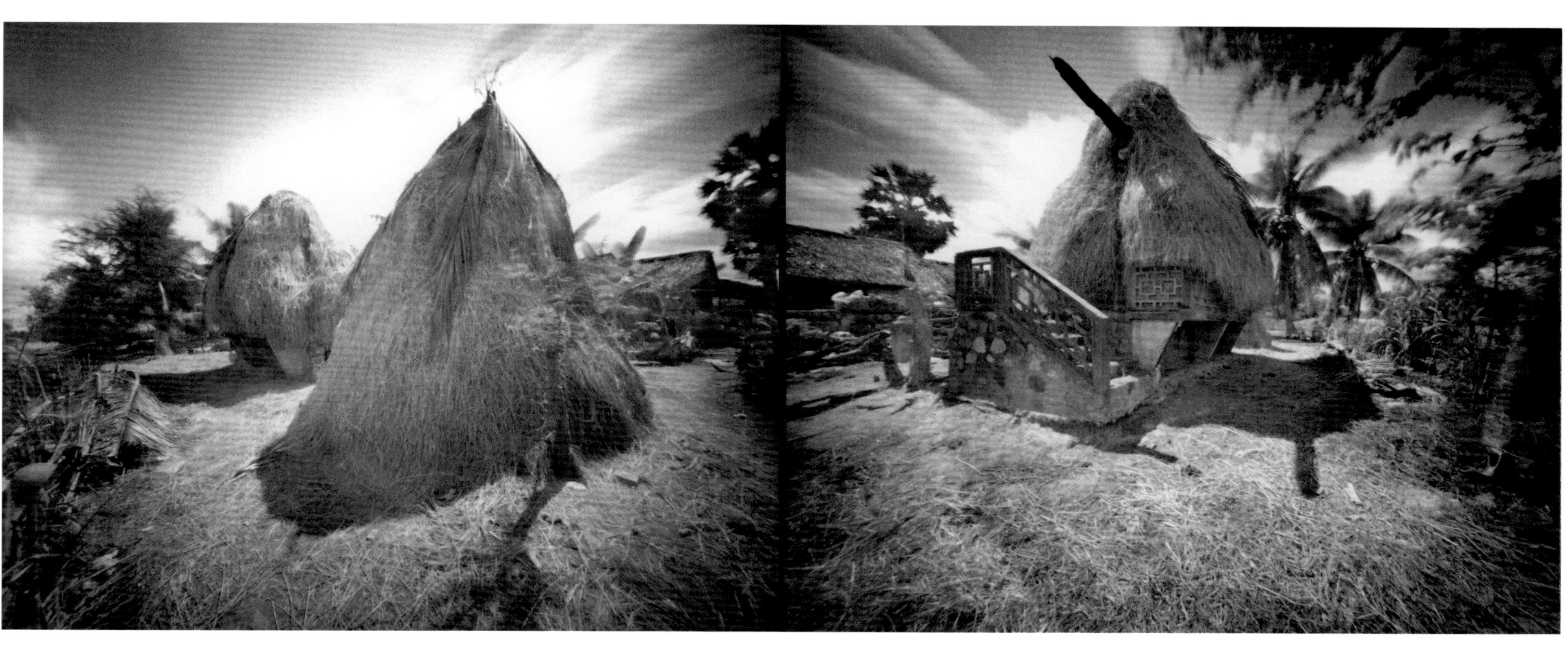

Plate 43

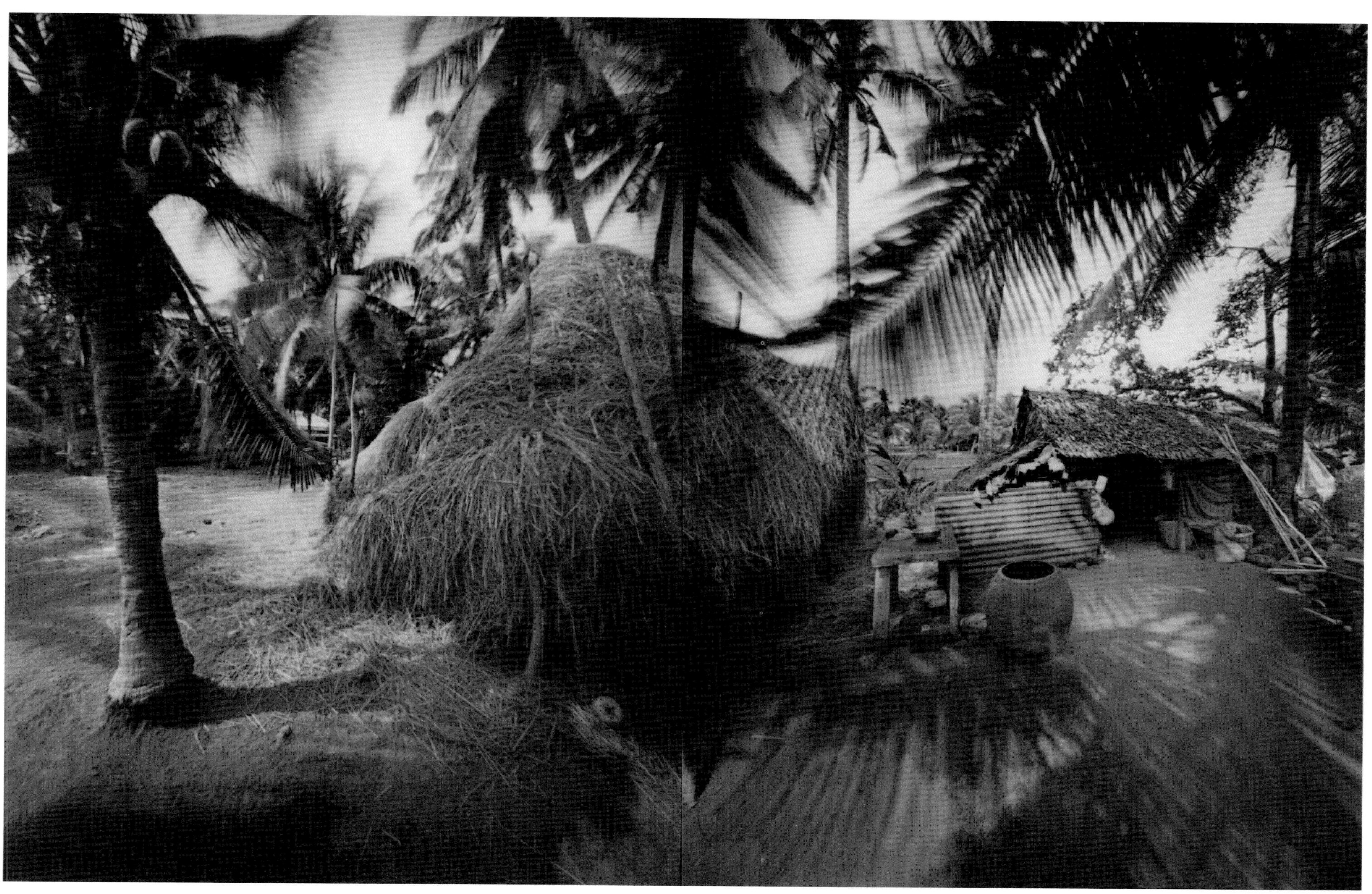

Plate 44

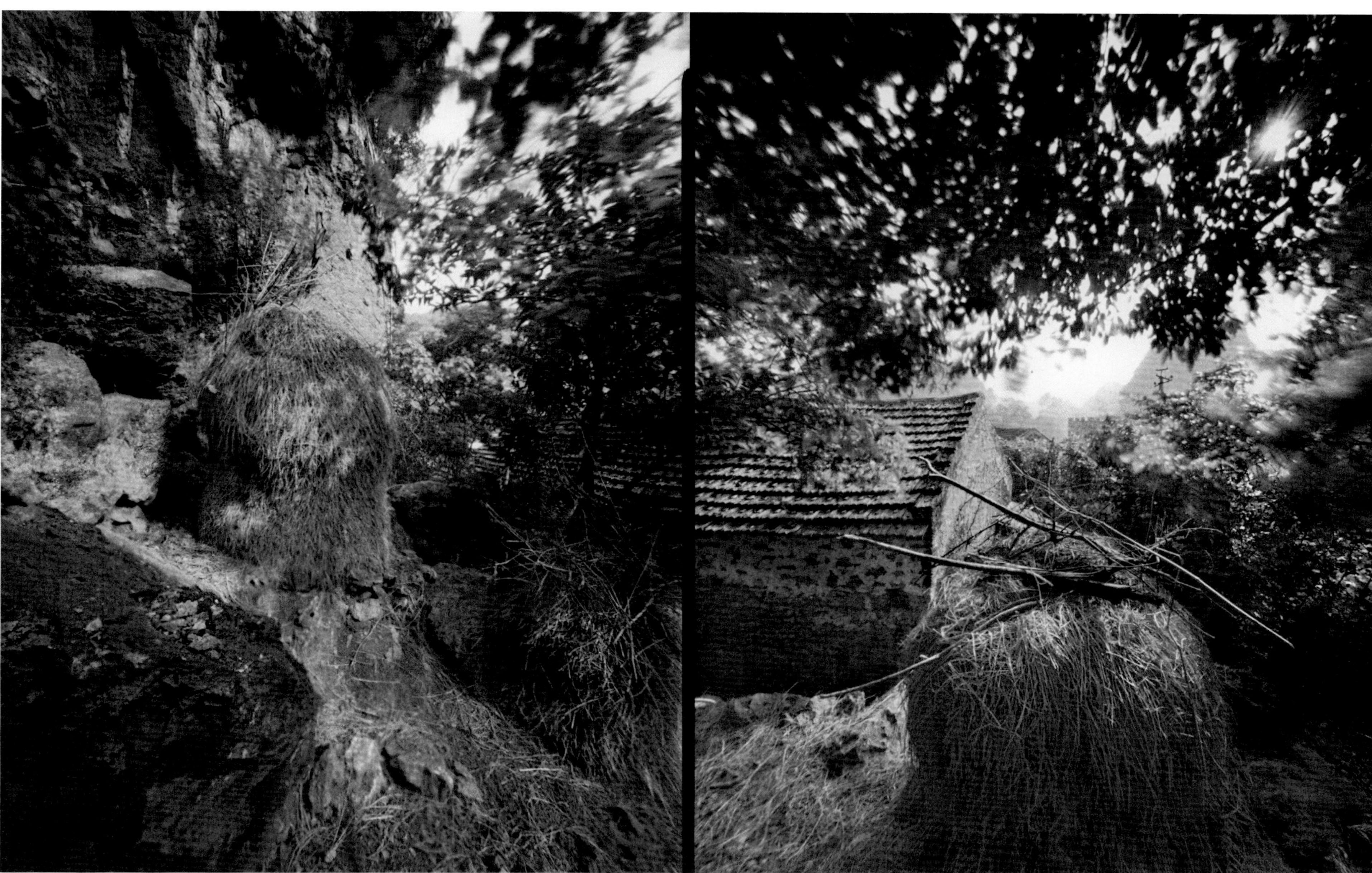

Plate 45

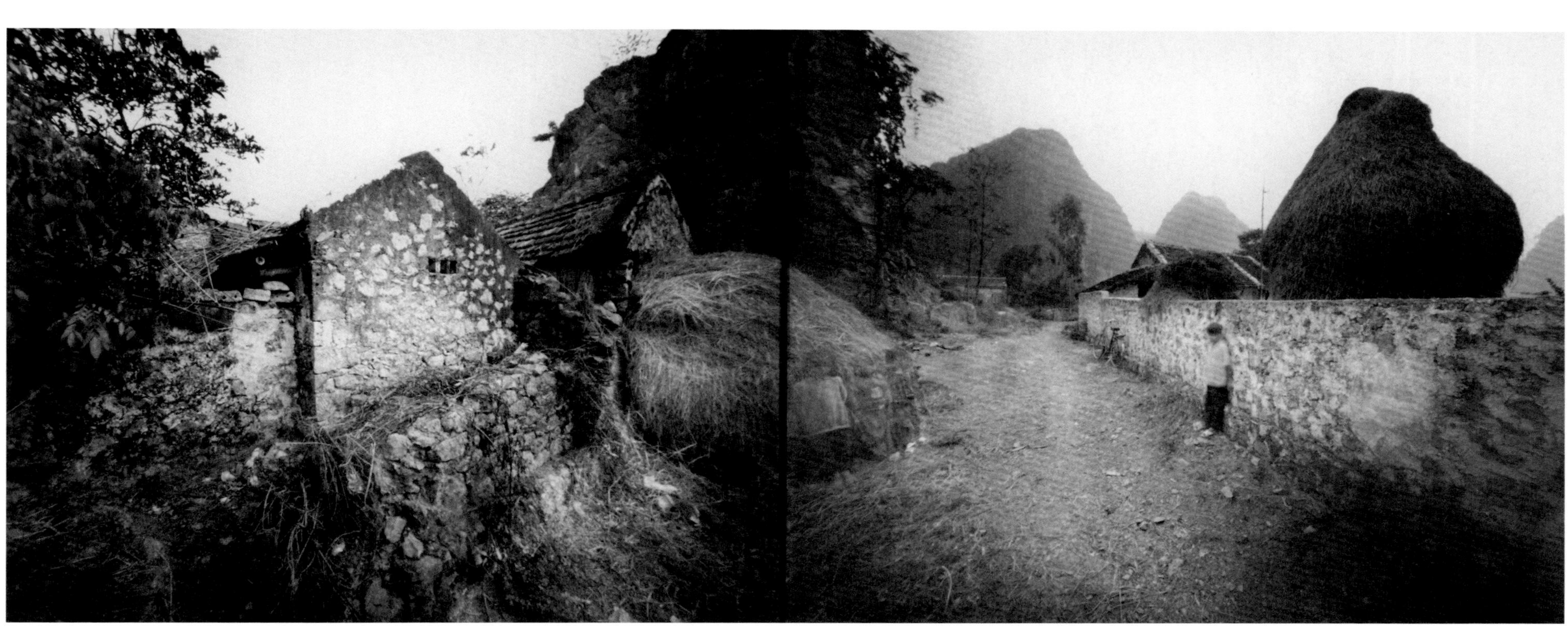

Plate 46

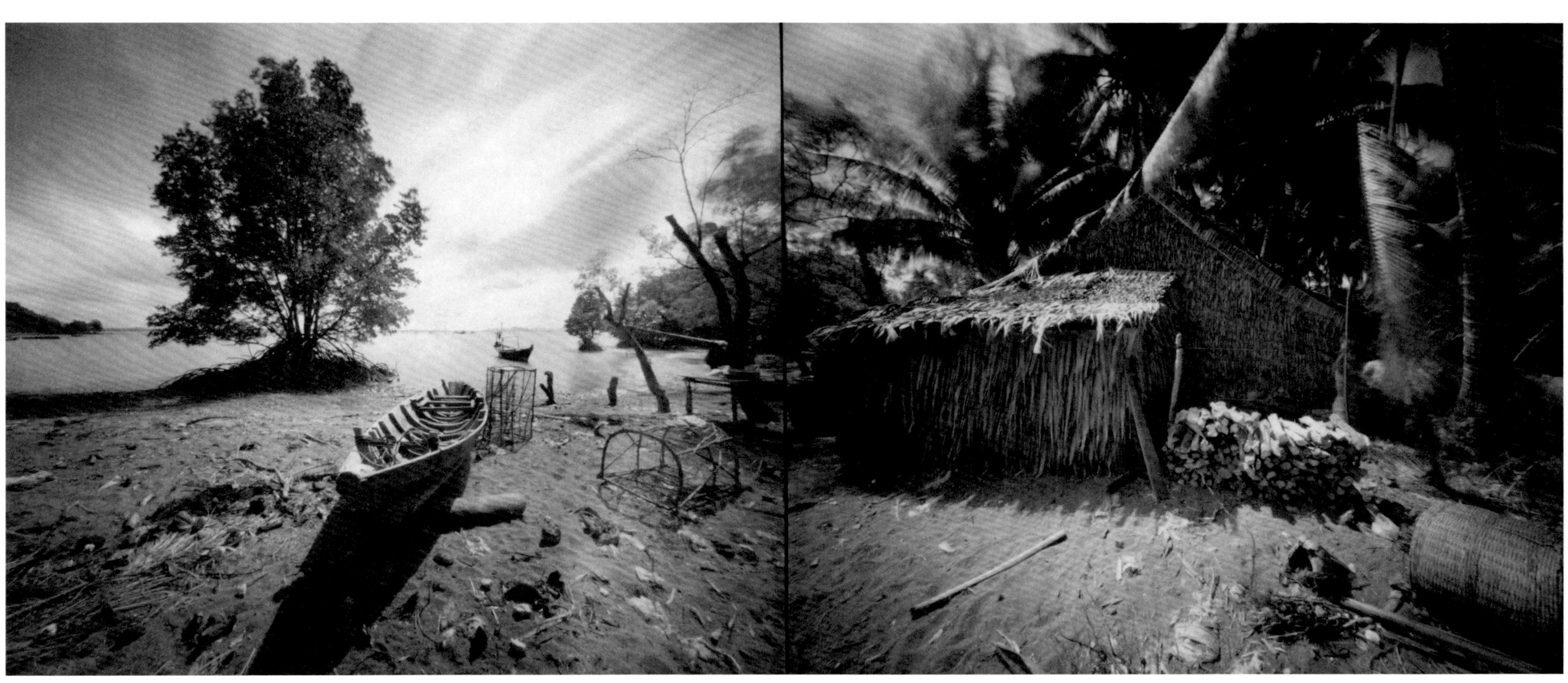

MY JOURNEY

by Craig J. Barber

The plane jostles back and forth in heavy turbulence as we descend through thick rain clouds. The country appears below me as a giant quilt of rice paddies and vegetable plots. The sky is gray, the runway gray, the terminal gray. We touch down on the tarmac in a vigorous rain. The rain. Of course. In my memories it is always raining in Vietnam.

The airport appears to have been built in the finest Soviet tradition—all concrete, no frills. The air is thick with the smell of diesel. We are unceremoniously loaded onto spartan gray buses and then ushered into the terminal where, in spite of the fact that we all have visas, we are required to fill out visa applications. The taxi into Hanoi drives past endless rice paddies. I remember patrolling along dikes like these. Endless patrols.

Looking for a room in Hanoi, a Vietnamese man approaches and offers assistance. I feel the normal hesitation anyone feels when approached by a stranger in a foreign country but, for a moment, I feel something more than that, something that is about memory. The last time I was here, you couldn't trust anybody. I feel an echo of that past conditioning, even though I know better. I recover quickly and decide to accept his offer. The room he helps me secure is clean and very nice.

Roaming around the city. Streets teeming with life, handcarts overflowing, women shouldering double loads under conical straw hats, crowded sidewalk markets, flowers, fresh fruit, hot pastries, horns blaring, old Soviet trucks lumbering and belching, cyclo-drivers pedaling everywhere, a few cars, plenty of motorcycles, and thousands of bicycles moving about in a frenzied mass. Amazingly no one seems to collide with anyone else, although men with repair patches and bicycle pumps await disaster. Inside a department store the effectiveness of the old U.S. embargo is painfully evident—limited goods behind unreachable counters, the walls, fixtures, tile floors all old, all fatigued.

I have not lied about being an American nor have I been rebuffed because of it. Quite the contrary. As I walk along the streets people nod in salutation. The children beg for money, young boys pop out of the woodwork with postcards, maps, phrase books for sale. I think of "Zeke," the little cigarette-smoking eight-year-old who was my buddy; helping me draw buckets of fresh water for bathing. The bathing area was hidden between giant boulders and a grove of banana trees near the base of our hill-top observation post. The compound nearby housed "mama-san" and "papa-san" (that's what we called them). The guys would rough-house with Zeke, throwing him into ponds or getting him drunk on sake, but there were many acts of compassion as well—food, medicine, clothes. We all seemed to enjoy each other's company, the kids and the jarheads. It was like older brothers picking on their younger siblings but happy to have them around. I wonder if Zeke survived. He would be in his thirties now. Would he recognize me? Would I recognize him?

When I think back, it's astounding that any of us survived. Land mines and sniper fire, machine gun ambushes and punji pits, mortar attacks and booby traps, red mud and the thick, wet heat. A Viet Cong village—six hours pinned down in a rice paddy, them shooting at us, us shooting at them. Unable to move, we call in air strikes. I mark the target with a Willy Peter round seventy-five yards away, jets so close I'm afraid my W.P. round will hit them. Bombs are dropped. Long, hot jagged pieces of shrapnel rain down around us. We lie flat against the ground and the earth trembles beneath our bodies as jets unload napalm. The noise, the heat, the smell! There are enormous holes where the village used to be. Tanks come to get our asses out. We ride the rear of the tank encrusted in thick red dust. Adrenaline rages! You got one, I got one. We kept score like it was a football game. It wasn't real. We were out of control. I felt invincible. I painted a bulls eye on my helmet as a dare. I was eighteen.

I need to get out of the city to photograph. The streets are far too crowded with moving objects for me to safely consider setting up my equipment. I go to Tran Quoc Pagoda where the scent of incense is in the air. At the "Temple of Literature," traditional folk music provides the background. As always, my working methods and strange black boxes attract substantial interest, and my appearance doesn't allow me to fade into the background. I'm six feet, six inches and I really stand out here. The Vietnamese are a petite people; most of the populace is half my size or less. I am an object of much scrutiny, not all of it polite. People grab my arm or my wrist as if measuring me, young men and boys run up alongside or behind me to compare themselves, or jump up and down in an effort to be eye-to-eye. I would like to be oblivious to this but it's not possible. Always a crowd gathers. As I look closer I realize there are some in the background whose eyes are not so welcoming. Older people, people who lived through the war.

The Army Museum, built after 1975 by the Vietnamese government to commemorate the victory of the people. I look at B-52 wreckage and the insides of a cluster bomb, seeing all the little bombs that are dispersed upon impact. The Vietnamese managed to force both France and the U.S. out of their country with punji spikes, pits and booby traps. They fought the French with bows and arrows. So many died. Now Vietnam is a land full of children. Fifty percent of their population was born after the fall of Saigon. Today I fell into conversation with three college students in the park. They had many questions for me, questions about music and computers. They are part of a generation that wants to move forward and engage the world, the U.S. included. For them the war is something taught in a history class.

Much to my surprise I discover the rusted remains of a 106 mm recoilless rifle, outside the tourist office of all places. Firing mechanisms have been stripped, probably by the U.S., and then abandoned. Damn. I remember firing those things, disassembling them, cleaning them, all of it. We spent two months with the Montagnards, the hill tribes who worked with us because they hated the Vietnamese. I remember guarding a river from high above and south of Quang Nhai. I was the gunner. We used special rounds that travel many hundreds of yards and then disperse small arrow pellets over a vast area. We kept that river clear of boats. A "free fire zone." Christmas and New Year's and Tet, firing away in a free fire zone. Merry Christmas to all and to all a dead night.

Moving farther out into the more remote countryside. The bamboo groves are beautiful, a rich, deep green. The wind makes an eerie sound blowing through the dense wood. The rivers and rice paddies support an abundance of bird life: snowy egrets, kingfishers, white cranes standing out in stark contrast to the lush green growth. I can't remember birds from before. Did we scare them away? Kill them off? I remember cats, dogs, rats, water buffalo, but not birds. Why can't I remember any birds? Maybe they were there and I just didn't see them. We were constantly moving, wet, hot, parched, hungry, full of pain, crazy, permanently pissed. Adrenaline kept us going. Wandering through a quiet village all those years ago, ten of us on recon-patrol, villagers smiling and waving. One hundred meters later all hell breaks loose. We're caught in a horseshoe-shaped machine gun ambush. Four of us are hit immediately. Our machine gunner takes out one of Charlie's positions. I'm at the other end, following suit with my weapon on another machine gun position. I'm standing up the whole time, shit flying everywhere. Again, I'm unscathed. The entire affair takes about twenty or thirty minutes. We retreat with no more casualties. As we move back through the previously "friendly" village, it's now empty. We feel suckered. We blow the village off the face of the earth.

The Vietnamese are not only fascinated by my size but also by my gray hair, blue eyes, earrings, fair skin, chest, and forearm hair. They pinch, grab, squeeze, and caress my arms, legs and ears. At lunch, a young girl came up, sat beside me, and proceeded to poke and probe wherever I allowed her. She even pulled up my pant leg to inspect my leg hair. Then, when I paid attention to her, she became shy and disappeared. Crowds of children show up, ever curious but reluctant to get too close. They push each other forward in the sacrificial manner of the Adele penguins with the leopard seal: if I don't devour the first child, they all venture forward. When these crowds are made up of children, this can be endearing, but at times I tire of the constant attention, and when I am trying to work it becomes intolerable.

In the cities, the "Modern" buildings look like the 1930's. Outside the cities there are times I feel as if it were the fourteenth century as I wander through the countryside, visiting the islands and small hamlets. They are deeply impoverished but incredibly efficient. For people here, hard labor from sunrise to sunset is a seven-day-a-week reality. So many of the working methods are primitive, yet perfected to optimum efficiency. An irrigation system employs a giant spoon swinging back and forth from holding pond to paddy. Two people, one at each end of a double rope, pull a bucket between them, dipping in and dumping out the water. Cabinet makers and boat builders do everything by hand, working in bare feet, oblivious to Western standards of safety. The resourcefulness of the Vietnamese is unending. Bomb craters have been turned into fish-rearing ponds, and watering reservoirs, metal sections from former airstrip runways are now window grates and fences, shell casings function as fence posts, canteen cups are common, a fifty-five gallon drum replaces a defunct radiator with a gravity drip system. Is it any wonder they beat the French and the U.S.?

If you exclude television, karaoke, and motorbikes, the thing that amazes me most about Vietnam is how little has changed since 1967. It looks the same, feels the same, smells the same. The lack of discernible change is jarring at times. Memory runs deep in my veins as I wind my way along narrow dirt paths and bamboo groves, past straw houses and barking dogs. More than once as I wander the small hamlets, I have felt on patrol, the weight of my pack reminiscent of those days and the tripod feeling like a weapon. But now I'm searching for images instead of "Charlie." These moments are disconcerting but I do not brush them aside. I am trying not to brush anything aside, I want to embrace all that comes along. The thought occurs to me that returning to Vietnam with so little changed after twenty-eight years is roughly equivalent to returning to a class reunion and finding your old friends unchanged—no wrinkles, no sages, no gray hair. But I have changed. My observational skills are better. My eye is keener, and the haste of youth is now tempered with the desire to observe, to engage, and embrace. Now I have the opportunity to do so. Then, of course, I didn't have the luxury of noticing. We were busy with other things.

The South China Sea. Today the sky is full of clouds and the temperatures have plunged. It's cold and windy. I go to the beach and watch turbulent waves pound in foamy fury. The tourists are elsewhere, even the hawkers and beggars are avoiding the thick gray sky and rambunctious sea. It's a delight to hear the crashing surf and to feel cool, a refreshing reprieve from the stifling heat. While leaving the beach I notice the lifeguard's tower and a small hut nearby. It reminds me of "C" Company camped in endless sand dunes. In those early days the patrols were light and friendships were easily made, before our lives turned crazy as we moved north. War brought us together and we cared for each other in ways I have not known since. We depended on each other, looked out for each other. The insanity was shouldered together. That was where Vic and I became buddies. We stayed in tents that housed eight to ten guys. Vic was assigned to the cot next to mine. We asked each other the usual questions. Where are you from? What's your family like? We hit it off immediately and became close friends. We made plans for what we were going to do when the war was over, when we got back to the States. We talked about going into business together, about going to school. His mom wrote to me, my mom wrote to him. The first time he was hit, I bandaged him up and put him on a chopper. The afternoon he returned from the hospital ship, we were just heading out for a night ambush and he asked if we would "wait up" because he wanted to join us. We thought he was nuts, but then again, we all were. We were a team.

Vic was killed while we were guarding bridges. I will never forget that night. Never. We'd been manning these bridges for about two weeks. Usually he and I would have been in the same place, but that night I was deployed down the road. His bridge was overrun by a company of North Vietnamese Army troops. I heard the whole thing on the radio. There was gunfire, then a rocket hit their bunker and a gasoline can exploded. They were pleading for help. Everyone inside was trapped and burned. Six guys died. We placed their remains in a one-pound coffee tin. I came to Vietnam a child. I left an old man.

Two women move a firewood wagon, one pushing, one pulling. The load is a strain, their faces bare their burden. All day, men and women bent at the waist work their rice paddies. A man stands up on a wooden plow, mud to his knees, a whip in one hand, reins in the other as a water buffalo pulls him back and forth, back and forth, across the paddy. Two men squat upon a large bamboo mat weaving a basket boat. They make the equivalent of a dollar a day. A man shovels sand from the river bottom, loads his small boat and rows his harvest ashore to market. Sand is moved from river to shore, from cart to construction site. A clay tile cutter produces tile after tile as a man methodically loads each one upon a gurney for two women who endlessly walk from cutter to drying yard with loads of bricks on each shoulder. As they fill the kiln, the men stack it all in place and light the fires that will harden the bricks. A woman squats at the edge of a wheel throwing large pots while another stands above, simultaneously kicking her partner's wheel and wedging the clay. They both look more than seventy years old. Mat weavers, boat builders, fishermen, farmers, net makers, postcard boys, begging children—such hard lives. I have heard tourists complain of paying more for items than the locals, of feeling ripped off and taken advantage of. They seem to feel they should be paying only what the Vietnamese pay, but I wonder if they want to earn a Vietnamese wage as well?

The trip from Hue to Hoi An covers familiar ground. I remember riding shotgun for a supply convoy from Da Nang to Phu Bai on this same road twenty-eight years ago. For us, it was a rare chance to relax and look at the countryside, a luxury. Usually we walked everywhere, dragging our butts through the rain and the mud. On this particular trip we caught a break; nothing eventful happened. We didn't get shot at, we got to ride in trucks, we watched the countryside go by, a little like what I'm doing now.

Hoi An is quiet, quaint, and delightful. I do not feel harassed here, quite the opposite. It's relaxing. The town's economy is a blend of fishing and agriculture, serving as a small urban supply center for the surrounding hamlets. The reception I have received has been friendly without the constant chorus of children begging and yelling, "Hello Money?" that follows foreigners everywhere. My first two evenings here are shared with fellow travelers, some Germans and some Americans. Substantive discussions, thought-provoking to be sure. My status as a vet certainly piques interest. Understandably, all want to know my response to being back and I tell the truth—it's good. All have questions regarding my experience, especially my having been a combat Marine. I share a few details but, as always, restrict most. I have been well received by fellow travelers, compassionately received, actually. Most seem to feel that my being here, now, is some sort of courageous act. To me it doesn't feel that way. Maybe I am downplaying this but I don't see it as such a big event. I admit I was nervous about returning but I wasn't afraid. I was ready. It has been possible to navigate the flood of memories I have encountered, all strong, all vivid with tremendous texture. Memories long buried, some trivial, some significant: I welcome them all. This is helping me to understand a part of myself. This is helping me appreciate who I was and who I have become.

I wish I had been wiser then. I wish I had been here on a different mission. We were armed and dangerous teenage boys in an exotic foreign land, confronting strange people and strange customs. We engaged in dubious hijinks out of sheer boredom: staged firefights complete with hand grenades and pyrotechnics, fraternity-style hazing, beer and pot, pot and beer. I was a kid from rural New York. I knew fishing and swimming, baseball and hockey, walking through woods where fresh winter snows blanketed the landscape revealing coon tracks and the occasional glimpse of deer and red fox. I knew nothing of what was to come when the killing began, when sheer survival became the overwhelming requirement—wounded Marines and dead civilians, wounded civilians and dead Marines.

"Thou shall not kill." I mean, get real, we were blowing each other up, for god's sake. I know others who felt the same way, like it was a dark adventure or some kind of insane game. In sports we award trophies, in war we award medals. The government kept score with their body counts, we kept score on the ground. We told and retold our battle stories: "Man, the shit hit the fan and I'm still here. Too bad about." When I think back now I realize all that was a way of relishing our own continued survival, but it was a strange life for kids. There were times I sank so low my heart hurts just thinking about it. Was it the will to survive or was I cold-blooded? Firefights made me feel alive. Life is no more vivid than when death is so near. And luck stayed with me. The day we strolled into a mine field it was hot, the air still, the grasses dry. Then the explosions began, the screams: five hit in front of me, five hit behind me. I didn't have a scratch. We bandaged everyone, the choppers arrived and took them away, we continued our patrol. Comrades wounded, killed, but not me. Why? How did I, the biggest target in all of Vietnam, continue to escape death?

I've been introduced to Hai, who comes enthusiastically recommended as a translator by the Americans I met when I first arrived in Hoi An. He is friendly, seems trustworthy, and is interested in what I am doing. We settle on a price. After working with him for one day, I know this is someone I can feel comfortable with.

Each day and each trip out of Hoi An reveals a new and equally exciting landscape. I move between closely placed bamboo mat homes winding around the edge of a lagoon, the paths defined by intricately woven bamboo fences, sunlight reflected through the groves on to the river's surface. Shrimp-rearing ponds intermingled with low-growing palms, fish traps creating watery "V's" across the lagoons, earthen dikes containing all. Here the intrusion of the curious is less than before but the children remain abundantly inquisitive. Hai is wonderful keeping them at bay during the critical minutes of exposure. There is the occasional feisty girl or boy who flaunts his commands—this is to be expected—but most are cooperative.

A stunning day. The afternoon light is fantastic, great patterns and definition. Photographing in a small fishing hamlet call An Hoi, we meet a young man curious about the strange American and wanting to practice his English. This happens a lot and can be distracting, but he is friendly and intelligent and today I welcome the engagement. He leads us through the maze of homes to his uncle's house where we are invited in for tea. His uncle is a painter and musician who, hearing of my interest in music, plays several songs on his guitar, accompanied by his wife on vocals. I am shown his paintings, some rather good. It is all very pleasant. Conversation turns to the inevitable. Was I here before 1975? Yes. In what region? In Chu Lai and Da Nang. The uncle looks at me with amazement and says, "I, too, fought in Chu Lai and Da Nang. I'm V.C." We stare at each other. Then we hug with great warmth, smiling, laughing. How happy we are that we did not kill each other, that the war is over, that we meet now, together, for tea and music.

Cam Ha—a small hamlet where people make bricks for their livelihood. Bamboo houses bump up against thatch roof-covered kilns. Sulfurous clouds spew forth, air burns the eyes, the lungs. Young and old labor throughout the day in the tropical heat. The entire town is clay, mud, and dust. Everything is tan: bricks, kilns, houses, legs, arms, life. Old women bent at the waist, hands and legs covered with coal dust, forming fuel bricks for the firings, a dreadful task, all day, every day, all their life. Men with shovels and water buckets dig and mix, dig and mix, women shape the bricks, children too. The town and environs are gradually sinking lower and lower as more and more clay is shaped, baked, and sold. Hai says the government wants to close the town's kilns because of the air pollution. What will these poor souls do? This is the life they were born to, it is all they have known for generations. The hardest part, apparently, is yet to come.

Binh Son on the Song Tra Bong (River). This village was my first experience of Vietnam. I remember playing with children, distributing the clothing my Mom sent, eating duck eggs and rice, the white sand, warm Cokes and hot skies, fishermen and fisherboys, sandbag bunkers and rats, makeshift poncho tents that leaked even in minor rains, boring guard duty and beautiful views, rice paddies, coconut trees and the South China Sea. Now I return to this same village. Much feels familiar: the sand, the curving river, rice paper drying under the hot sun, squid, fishermen, river nets and basket boats. Even a few faces are familiar. There are more brick homes and motorbikes and the village now ascends the hill the Marines called "Lima 2," where our unit was deployed. I can't believe people recognize me after all these years. An old woman comes up to say she remembers me, and then another approaches, and another and another. This is unexpected. People swarm around trying to place me and wanting to know if I remember so and so. Those old enough to remember me, do. Children, seeing an American for the first time, are curious. I am the first one, the only one, to return. I am a celebrity. Then I see Hanh. She remembers me well. She was sixteen and I was eighteen. She was one of the many who were warm and friendly towards us. She invites me to her home for tea and talk and to introduce me to her children who have all inherited her beautiful looks. At forty-five she still looks darn good. Her house is filled with visitors, stifling heat and no air, but all is well. She and I are all smiles, happy to see one another. The others, sensing our joy, immerse themselves in our feelings and make them theirs. It's like a party. Suddenly we are rudely interrupted by an army officer with "green" in his eyes. He marches us down to the river where we board a lorry and are sent across to the local headquarters of the Army of the People's Republic of Vietnam. There we are asked the standard questions, and Hai is required to promise in writing that he will never bring anyone into this area without a travel permit. The officer informs me that all of Vietnam is open except the spot we happen to be standing on. He then declares that Vietnam wants improved relations with the U.S., and promptly proceeds to extort money from me. He appears to have been drinking heavily. The affair drags on for hours. I have to restrain myself from laughing at the commandant's "improved relations" comment—in view of his conduct I'm glad he doesn't want bad relations. He claims the locals have painful memories of the Marines which I find rather curious considering the outpouring of glee I have just experienced. The travel permit story doesn't wash either. The entire event is a sham. I'm just a quick buck. Hai is nervous knowing how miserable the authorities can be but my chief concern is my film. I'm worried they might confiscate my work. Thank God it doesn't come to that. The whole affair transpires in the usual fatigued building crying out for a coat of paint, pictures of Marx, Lenin, and Ho Chi Minh staring down from the peeling walls, the troops with more stars and stripes on their shoulder boards than there are on some flags. All in all, we were lucky, and I did get to see the other side of the river and was finally able to ride in one of the basket boats—always wanted to do both. Taken altogether, it was great day.

I talk to a well-educated man with excellent English skills and a desire to speak frankly about Vietnam and its relations with the U.S. Much of what he has to say is right on the mark and grounded in the reality of daily life. He describes the mess that existed between 1975 and 1990; the oppressive dictatorship of the Communists and the folly of their policies; the fall of the Soviet Union and Eastern Europe and their collective impact upon the leadership of Viet Nam. He speaks of the need for U.S. assistance in rebuilding their war-ravaged land and economy. We made a mess here and we need to help clean it up. I cannot argue with the man; I agree with him. The bigger questions remain: why did we ever go to war with these people, bomb this land, this culture? They will never recover from the level of destruction, deforestation, desecration, and toxic poisoning they have suffered. What did we need to achieve? What did we achieve?

The Nguyen Hue Café, a favorite place. Gentle breezes and sheltering shade, shops on one side and an elegant old colonial building in serious disrepair gracing the other. At road's end, the river. Life flows by and shadows dance across the pages of my journal. The couple who run this quiet spot are young, warm, friendly, and generous. They always greet me with inviting smiles and warm words.

Hai has proven to be a very helpful assistant and a good companion. Yesterday afternoon he confessed to me how much he enjoys the work I do and exploring all the areas we have wandered through. Apparently he has, for the first time, stopped to "see." We are becoming friends, as I am with a number of others in this community. Genuine affection has developed between us. This heightens my experience here. I see not only the beauty of this country but of its people as well. Like people everywhere, some are ignorant and rude, some are extraordinarily sweet, intelligent, wonderful. Each day becomes a revelation, each revelation a warm embrace for my soul, each embrace an act of healing.

It's early morning in Hoi An. Shopkeepers and cafe owners are busy preparing for their day. Women shuffle by with marketable goods suspended in dual baskets balanced upon bamboo poles. A man riding his bicycle has several ducks lashed together and draped over his handlebars, each very much alive and quacking their displeasure over such treatment. School girls walk hand-in-hand, boys do, too. A pig finds itself strapped across the rear of a bicycle in a body-gripping basket of woven bamboo, on its way to the morning market. Two women push and pull an overloaded cart burdened with firewood. Children run and shriek. Old people beg. A war veteran, through years of practice, balances himself by placing his left leg stump through his crutch and lopes along at a surprising pace. An enterprising woman chomping on a cigarette, stakes a claim to one section of the sidewalk, transforming it into a motorbike parking lot where she watches over her charges for a modest fee. The bicyclists alone are worth the price of admission. There are men who sit behind the seat, on the fender, to pedal. Couples help each other pedal, two feet on each pad. Young boys standing on the luggage rack while their father pedals. Babies in baskets. Little girls whose feet don't quite reach, yet they know just how to time their foot movement so as to push only at the top of the cycle. The small boy who stands to pedal while performing a delicate balancing act below the cross bar, all back-dropped by the time-worn ocher buildings and coconut trees of this vibrant, teeming community.

In Paul Theroux's Riding the Iron Rooster, he quotes Mao Zedong: "All genuine knowledge originates in direct experience." These words could not better describe my feelings about this journey. Yesterday, as Hai and I visited a Buddhist pagoda in Cam Ha, I thought again about how little we knew or understood while occupying this country. Of course, had we identified with Vietnam or with the Vietnamese, we would not have been such willing participants in their destruction. Now I receive "genuine knowledge," some of it great, some of it not, but all of it real. The warmth I receive, and the fortitude of these people, cannot help but win over all but the hardest of hearts.

Hai and I make our way back to the Cham towers outside Tam Ky. Three haystacks are juxtaposed against three towers. Good light and great patterns. En route we also make a couple of exposures in Tam An and stop at a farm house in Que Cuong where the final products of the sugar harvest are stacked and arranged in intriguing shapes and forms. It is picturesque but it is the result of impoverished lives, hard lives. Behind the stunning shapes and extraordinary light is the horrendous residue of war and the harsh reality of poverty. Most Americans know next to nothing about Vietnam except for B-52's and napalm, My Lai and drugs. I want my work to bring a new chapter of information to the "Walter Cronkite" generation, those who consumed the latest body count with their evening meal. Vietnam is a complex mixture of beauty and difficulty, of resilience and determination. It is a unique realm. I hope the images I have made are worthy of this place, expressing that singular beauty and my feelings for it.

The warmth and friendship I have received is a tremendous comfort. My heart is healing and I feel more peaceful than I have in years, perhaps ever. It is time to heal, not only for the veterans of the war but for all of us. It is time for us to learn about this culture, this land, these people. The ghosts in the Vietnam landscape haunt America to this day. It is time to put our ghosts to rest.

I am deeply involved with Viet Nam. I am captured by it. Haunted by all of the death, I cry for those whose lives I witnessed lost and for those whose loss of life I caused. There was cruelty, evil, and horror. The pain is forever. There are times I am afraid. There are times I am angry. There are times I just sit and let the tears flow. But coming here was not only the right thing, it was one of the smartest things I've ever done. Before it was about death and dying, kill or be killed. It was totally crazy. Now it is about learning, caring and forgiving. Now it is about seeing.

Steep mountains, emerald paddies, coconut oasis, lush bamboo, ancient temples, straw houses, crumbling colonial mansions, haystacks and water buffalo, television sets in dirt-floored huts, blackened teeth and sweltering heat, crystal blue skies and cool lagoons, terrible pain and senseless loss, delicate beauty and a resilient spirit. Vietnam.

PLATES

ACKNOWLEDGMENTS

This is a book about healing and my journey to catharsis.

As with all journeys, you must take the initial first step and mine was made easier by Dianne Banser, Sally Hanna, Pam Horner and Wayne Lee. Without these friends and the open hearts they gave me (without judgment) this journey would have been a much rougher road.

My profound thanks to the many friends and colleagues who have given me guidance and moral support for my work throughout the years: Dan Burkholder, Stefano Campanini, Xavier Canoone, Connie Coleman, Sam Dickerson, Penny and Gary Ferguson, Roy Flukinger, Keith A. Gasser, Gail Gibson, Ted Hartwell, Marita Holdaway, Jeffrey Hoone, Brooks Johnson, Anne Arden MacDonald, Warren Padula, Chris Rauschenberg, Andreas Rentsch, Robin Rice, Mark Sloan, Mary Virginia Swanson, Tom Toperzer, Wendy Watriss and Fred Baldwin, Lloyd Weller, and Marco Zecchin.

In Vietnam, my new Vietnamese friends embraced me and helped me learn about their land and their culture. Their warmth and openness was instrumental in the healing of old wounds. I would like to thank Ha and Chin for their incredible friendship. Most especially, I would like to thank Hai, for without his constant guidance, companionship, translation skills, patience, suggestions for which paths to follow and steady motorcycle driving skills, none of this would have happened. But mostly I would like to thank Hai for his friendship.

Additional gratitude goes to my many collectors and to the New York Foundation for the Arts who believed in this project and helped finance my expeditions to Southeast Asia.

I would also like to thank Melody Bostick and Richard Sullivan and the entire staff at Bostick & Sullivan Photo for their friendly advice and material support which helped make both the images in this book and the accompanying exhibition possible.

This book is the result of Nan Richardson's interest and commitment to my photography, Patricia Anderson's intelligent and thoughtful editing, and Dion Ogust's and Jeff Moran's willingness to read and re-read multiple drafts. The elegant design is the work of Tanja Geis whose sensitivity towards my vision was never in doubt and always appreciated. I'd also like to thank Amy Deneson and everyone at Umbrage Editions who helped bring *Ghosts in the Landscape* into the world.

To Alison Nordström I give my profound gratitude for her friendship and steadfast belief in both me and my work and for her eloquent and insightful writing about Vietnam and my images.

Finally, to my family, Ken and Ellie Barber, Keith Barber, Katryna Barber, and Roslyn McMurray for their support and for always believing in my mission.

Ghosts in the Landscape: Vietnam Revisited

An Umbrage Editions Book

First Edition

ISBN 1-884167-53-5

An Umbrage Editions book

Editor and Publisher: Nan Richardson
Managing Director: Amy Deneson
Director of Design and Production: Tanja Geis
Editorial Assistant: Emma Bedard
Copy Editor: Rebecca Bengal
Design Assistants: Erin Harley and Cecilia Ziko

Umbrage Editions, Inc.
515 Canal Street #4
New York, New York 10013
www.umbragebooks.com

This publication is accompanied by a national traveling exhibition organized by George Eastman House, International Museum of Photography and Film. The exhibition will go to the following venues: Griffin Museum, Winchester, Massachusetts, George Eastman House, Rochester, New York.

Distributed by Consortium
www.cbsd.com

Distributed by Turnaround Publisher Services in Europe
www.turnaround-uk.com

Printed in Italy